F. Tupper Saussy

THE MIRACLE ON MAIN STREET
Saving Yourself and America From Financial Ruin

SPENCER
JUDD,
PUBLISHERS
SEWANEE, TENNESSEE 37375

THE MIRACLE ON MAIN STREET

I get my greatest pleasure just being with my wife and family, playing and working with our children, writing an occasional song or piece of theatre, making watercolor pictures, being with sympathetic friends, and travelling. I don't get any pleasure whatsoever obeying statutes that don't apply to me. I have discovered, since becoming familiar with the Constitution, that a great many statutes do NOT apply to me, and my obedience to them is entirely optional.

People who know their rights and privileges under the Constitution of the United States are almost always able to prevent legal tangles by just showing a potential adversary the applicable section of the Supreme Law. That's all there is to it. Moreover, the Supreme Court has held time and again that "where the Constitution is clear, **it means what it says**," which is another way of saying "Don't waste the Court's time begging for interpretations; let the Constitution be your law."

Like many people in the past couple of decades, I taught myself how to play the guitar. In the same way, I am teaching myself the United States Constitution. It's the most exciting course in self-improvement you can take! In the four years I've been reading this document I'm continually discovering wonderful new authorities I can claim upon life. Probably the most rewarding thing of all, though, is the effect living by the Constitution has upon children.

Copyright 1980 by
SPENCER JUDD, PUBLISHERS
ALL RIGHTS RESERVED

Library of Congress Catalog Card No.: 80-52800

    Saussy, F. Tupper
      The Miracle on Main Street.
    Sewanee, Tenn.: Spencer Judd
    155 p.
    8008   800709
Manufactured in the United States
First Printing, 1980
Second Printing, February 1981
Third Printing, May 1981

CONTENTS

PROLOGUE: EXODUS FROM THE IDEASPHERE .. 5
1: THE GATHERING TRAGEDY 11
2: THE ONLY CAUSE OF INFLATION 17
3: THE RIGHT TO ALTER AND ABOLISH 23
4: A FAVOURABLE CRISIS FOR CRUSHING PAPER MONEY 27
5: A SUDDEN SENSE OF PROSPERITY AND TRANQUILLITY 35
6: WEAVERS OF "THE AMERICAN DREAM": THE FRIENDS OF PAPER MONEY 41
7: BROTHER MAX 47
8: IS DREAM MONEY LAWFUL MONEY? 53
9: STARTING THE MIRACLE BY REDUCING THE IGNORANCE FACTOR 59
10: THE PROPER COURSE FOR GOVERNMENT ... 67
11: UNDER INVESTIGATION 71
12: PUTTING THE CONSTITUTION INTO YOUR EVERYDAY CONVERSATION 77
13: A LESSON THEY'LL NEVER FORGET 85
14: THE MIRACLE ON MAIN STREET 91
15: UNDERSTANDING GOVERNMENT FOR WHAT IT REALLY IS 103
EPILOGUE: THE ILLUSION OF STATUS QUO 109
APPENDIX 117

FOREWORD

Distinguished economics experts, Nobel prize winners, and White House advisors notwithstanding, THE MIRACLE ON MAIN STREET contains *the only lawful and workable solution there can ever be to our worsening financial woes, public and private.* Amazingly, this solution is already with us, built into the mechanics of our government. But the design is such that the solution must be activated from OUTSIDE government, activated by you and me—the people. The reason the solution has lain dormant for so long is that the people have *somehow* been kept unaware of the presence of the solution. *Until this book.*

Tupper Saussy goes right to the Supreme Law of the Land to reveal that solution to us. Then, he shows step by step how the solution will be *achieved*. As each individual uses the United States Constitution to preserve the value of his own fortune, our decaying federal economic, political, and social conditions will begin healing themselves literally over-night. This truly is the stuff of which miracles are made.

—James A. Woods, *P.E.,*
Engineering Consultant; Director,
Franklin County (TN) Taxpayers
Association

For my wife, Frédérique.

With special thanks to
the good people of Robertsville and the Porths, Harmons,
Rielys,
Christensens, Cooleys, Ellsworths, and Schiffs:
the most powerful and least harmful of all Americans.

THE MIRACLE ON MAIN STREET

"*From* 80 to 90% of the population can be hypnotized to varying degrees. . . . At least 5% (10,000,000) of the U.S. population is extraordinarily hypnotizable, so easily hypnotizable that they are in a constant state of exaggerated suggestibility, even when awake and going about their normal daily routine. They are at the TOTAL MERCY of all forms of influences and can easily be persuaded to do things and afterward have no idea why they did them . . . They go in and out of a trance-like state without even knowing what is happening to them. As a result, they suffer all kinds of problems without realizing the real cause."

—Dr. Tobias H. Brocher,
Director, Center for
Applied Behavioral Sciences,
Menninger Foundation,
Topeka, Kansas in
National Enquirer, January 2,
1979

"*T*he destruction of a mighty nation may well be approaching because of the activities of one person. He has encouraged leaders to tranquillize the populace with halftruths. He has lured the press into inattention and has assisted the people in duping themselves. He has persuaded his fellow citizens to concentrate on life's comic strips and mindless entertainments and to avoid the bruises of reality.

"The culprit is the person whose eyes scan these words, and whose hands—at this moment—hold this book."

—William J. Lederer,
A Nation of Sheep, 1961

"*D*reams are for those who sleep."

—David Gates

PROLOGUE

EXODUS FROM THE IDEASPHERE

We put a lot of faith in ideas. So much faith that we're moved by them. Our motor nerves are tuned to the *ideasphere*. We think life consists of choosing the best idea from the selection offered and then living by it.

We forget that the ideasphere exists only in the mind. The mind is just a part of the whole individual, meaning that living by ideas deprives the rest of one's self of many pleasures it was born capable of feeling. Recently, a news story appeared in the world press about 14 Chinese children who could read with their skin. They could tell color blindfolded, by touching. Doctors were amazed and puzzled. And then there's all the documentation of ESP, clairvoyance, astral projection, telekenesis, and so on. The scientists who have sunk their lives into studying them maintain these phenomena are not weird but quite natural. Ordinary. They are merely abilities we all are born with in order to sense this world fully and live comfortably in it as participating organisms.

But beginning in our earliest years and continuing through our lifetime, these wonderful abilities are chased off into disuse by swarms of ideas. Ideas that we are somehow "bad," or "good," or "Mouseketeers," or "Peppers," or "cereal lovers," or "kids," or "mentally ill," or "Democrats," or "Republicans," or "Senior Citizens." Where do these ideas come from? *From those who profit by people's not using their natural abilities, where else?* From those who stake claims of authority over helpless people. From those who are in the *business* of guiding and governing others.

It's easy to see that if you can hook someone on an idea, on a dream, you can fleece his pockets. Reality overrules an idea every time. To keep control over people, you must keep the ideasphere charged with images, hopes, suggestions, debates and alternatives the same way radio fills the atmosphere with music and pulse. While the victim's lost in his dream, you can march stealthily into his fortunes and take what you want. With ideas, you can make him happy or afraid, make him dance or prefer one product to another. You can make him kill or build bomb shelters.

But for all ideas can make us do, they are only *ideas*. Dreams. I spent two terrified years in grammar school fearing graduation to Junior High School because of the hazing I would undergo. The ideasphere resounded with tales of 7th graders getting heads shaved and faces painted with red lipstick stripes, being forced to push B-B's down the highway with their noses, having to eat rotten eggs, having to walk home naked from some lonely spot in the woods. I suffered countless nightmares in apprehension of the coming of My Day. But when my day came, nobody did anything to me. I went through hazing without so much as a lovetap from an upperclassman. After hazing week was over, I almost felt . . . unwanted.

What had happened? I know now that I had *withdrawn* from the ideasphere at hazing time. When a hazer would come near me, there would be no transmission of look or feeling between us. No connection. Because hazing was an idea, he could only pick up from *subscribers* to the idea. *Believers*. He could attack only those whose eyes said "Please don't haze me." Eyes that asked "What's hazing?"

were ignored. They were not part of the ideasphere. They were of another frequency completely. Another world.

This was one of my earliest lessons in the utter fraudulence of ideas and has often been the manner in which I have approached problems.

This little book is not about ideas, except to encourage you to shun them. I hope it will wean you away from the ideasphere. This book is about a genuine, real thing you can touch. The difference between an idea and a thing you can touch was illustrated tragically to me years ago when a friend of mine, on LSD, thought he was pulling the trigger of a water pistol aimed at his temple but it was a loaded Colt .45. Ideas have their validity, but they're no match for reality. Reality overrules every time. (That's why these days I find it so hard to appreciate fiction. So much of what passes for reality is fiction enough!)

The reality of this book is: IF YOU DON'T LIKE WHAT'S HAPPENING IN YOUR LIFE, YOU CAN FIX IT. You can fix it without cheating anyone, without counselling with experts, without subscribing to any newsletter that keeps you posted on inside info, without writing Washington or getting involved in politics, without organizing, and without spending a penny unless you choose to.

And a miracle will happen: as you fix what's wrong in your OWN life, you'll automatically be fixing what's wrong with America's well-being. Instantly, you'll begin claiming your little-known and completely legal economic rights good for hundreds even thousands of extra dollars in your family treasury, and not applying to government for it, either! Couldn't you use some extra cash in these raw times? The law provides benefits for you, regardless of your age, condition, financial status, sex, or whatever. Benefits to help you survive the ups and downs and starts and jolts of this fluctuating economy. But if you continue swirling about in the weightlessness of ideas you'll never know how to claim these benefits. No, to experience THIS miracle, you must be down to earth.

I've shown this manuscript to people who can be counted on for merciless feedback. Any one of them could have halted publication simply by responding with faint praise. But the unanimous verdict seems to be "At last, a book that describes the problem and then gives a DIRECT, QUICK, NATURAL SOLUTION." I believe in direct, quick, natural solutions. I believe that when you have a mosquito bite, you should scratch it, not take Milk of Magnesia. Trying to solve one's own personal financial dilemma by appealing to the ideasphere—government, federations, organizations, advisors, financial planners, experts—is *submitting to surgery* for that mosquito bite. A sad, tragic waste of time, resources, and happiness.

I hope judges and mayors and court clerks and all levels of government employees will read this little book, because it was written as much for them as for people out of government. I hope bankers and reporters and small businessmen and schoolteachers will read it. And attorneys, who call themselves our guardians of the law. And housewives. Especially housewives and mothers. I hope church folks will read it, too, because after all God is the foundation of all miracles, including the restoration of a happy America. I cannot describe how vividly God progressed in me from an idea to a touchable reality as this book developed. Perhaps you will sense it as you read on.

Dream worlds are hard to leave. Even *painful* dream worlds are hard to leave. They're especially hard to leave when the dream makers tell us that leaving the dream world will be catastrophic. Many people actually *prefer* the ideasphere to reality, not caring that they are denying their whole selves pleasures of incredible intensity, pleasures and abilities truly "undreamed of." These people, and they are among our most respected citizens, are fully trained to believe in the life broadcast in the ideasphere, and they believe it can't get much better than it is. They'll never come around to reality until they must.

This little book can only switch on the lights for people

who are already tossing and turning under a terrifying yet fascinating nightmare. Suddenly, you bolt awake and there are your walls, the pictures, the lamps, the quilt, the soft breathing of your family. What had been twisting your body and mind was nothing but ideas, and they scamper away as soon as you open your eyes to the glowing warmth of the real world.

We don't need to *restore* the American Dream; we need to *wake up* from it.

"Thou shalt not have in thy bag divers weights, a great and a small. Thou shalt not have in thine house divers measures, a great and a small. But thou shalt have a perfect and just weight, a perfect and just measure shalt thou have: that thy days may be lengthened in the land which the Lord thy God giveth thee."
—Deuteronomy 25: 13-15

"The world has always been betrayed not by scoundrels but by decent men with bad ideas."
—Sydney J. Harris

"By a continuing process of inflation, governments can confiscate, secretly and unobserved, an important part of the wealth of their citizens. There is no subtler, no surer means of overturning the existing basis of society than to debauch the currency. The process engages all the hidden forces of economic law on the side of destruction, and does it in a manner which not one man in a million is able to diagnose."
—John Maynard Keynes,
The Economic Consequences of The Peace, 1920

1
THE GATHERING TRAGEDY

*B*lood running in the streets. Mobs of rioters and demonstrators threatening banks and legislatures. Looting of shop and home. Credit ruined. Strikes and unemployment. Trade and distribution paralyzed. Shortages of food. Bankruptcies everywhere. Court dockets overloaded. Kidnappings for heavy ransom. Sexual perversion, drunkenness, lawlessness rampant . . .

One distinguished politician writes to another: "The wheels of government are clogged, and we are descending into the vale of confusion and darkness. No day was ever more clouded than the present. We are fast verging to anarchy and confusion."

Where, when and whom? Get ready for a shock: *America*, 1786, ten years after the signing of the Declaration of Independence. The correspondence was from George Washington to James Madison. On February 3, 1787, Washington wrote to Henry Knox: "If any person had told me that there would have been such formidable rebellion as exists, I would have thought him fit for a madhouse." [1]

What went wrong? What forced this noble new country

---

1. This and all Washington quotations: Harry Atwood: *The Constitution Explained*, Destiny Publishers, Merrimac, Massachusetts, 1927, 1962.

into conditions far worse than the tyranny against which it had declared its independence in the first place? The history books tell us it was a complicated variety of interrelated things, but reality tells us it was only one: the money issued by the Continental Congress and the states' banking houses was paper that could not be redeemed for gold or silver coin. Inflation, *that* was what had sunk George Washington to the depths of despair.

The paper currency of the Congress was printed in such exorbitant amounts (in relation to the precious metals they represented) that wages and prices skyrocketed, forcing the Legislature to enact harsh wage and price controls. When these failed, moral-sounding laws reeking of piety and patriotism were enacted in an attempt to chain the people under penalty of violence to the government's absurd money:

> If any person shall hereafter be so lost to all virtue and regard for his Country as to refuse to accept its notes, such person shall be deemed an enemy of his Country.[1]

This amounts to a law protecting bad-check artists, and so the people naturally ignored it and others like it. The depreciation of paper currency relative to coin followed the same sickening course our paper currency follows today. (At this writing, the 1980 paper dollar is redeemable for a silver dollar at about 15 or 16 to 1.)

DEPRECIATION OF CONTINENTAL CURRENCY AGAINST THE SPANISH MILLED DOLLAR, 1779[2]

January 14 .... 8 to 1
February 3 .... 10 to 1
April 2 .... 17 to 1
May 5 .... 24 to 1
June 4 .... 20 to 1
September 17 .... 24 to 1
October 14 .... 30 to 1
November 17 .... 38 to 1

---

1. Davis R. Dewey: *Financial History of the United States*, John Wilson & Son, Cambridge, Mass. 12th Edition, 1934, pp 36 *et seq.*
2. *Ibid.*

In January, 1781, these notes were redeemable 100 to 1; in May, 1781, they ceased passing as currency and quietly died in the hands of their owners. Repeatedly, new series were issued, only to follow a similar pattern.[1]

A contemporary of the Revolution, Peletiah Webster, records it this way:

> It ceased to pass as currency (in May, 1781), but was afterwards bought and sold as an article of speculation, at very uncertain and desultory prices, from 500 to one thousand to one.[2]

Yet another contemporary writer, Breck, gives us this ridiculous aspect of inflation's ultimate achievement in the 1780's:

> The annihilation was so complete that barber-shops were papered in jest with the bills; and the sailors, on returning from their cruises, being paid off in bundles of this worthless money, had suits of clothes made of it, and with characteristic lightheartedness turned their loss into a frolic by parading through the streets in decayed finery which in its better days had passed for thousands of dollars.[3]

Again, Peletiah Webster writes:

> Paper money polluted the equity of our laws, turned them into engines of oppression, corrupted the justice of our public administration, destroyed the fortunes of thousands who had confidence in it, enervated the trade, husbandry, and manufactures of our country, and went far to destroy the morality of our people.[4]

Describing inflation to someone who has never experienced it is like describing the pain of fire to someone who has never been burned. You really have to live it to know how terrible it is. More than one Biblical scholar who has felt inflation concludes that the Beast in Revelation is nothing less than inflation itself. The worst thing about inflation is that there are so many *apparent* causes of it. The

---
1. *Ibid.*
2. *Ibid.*
3. *Ibid.*
4. *Ibid.*

long-winded debate over *cause* only gives inflation time to spread and destroy more. The debate over cause is usually conducted by the many people who *benefit* from inflation, those who are first in line from the printing press, able to buy goods at current prices with money that soon raises the price of everything as it goes into circulation, increasing the volume of the money supply. It doesn't take much digging to know who the first-in-liners are: they're the beneficiaries of government programs and, of course, the beneficiaries of our bank system. Which is a whole lot of people, very few of whom are going to want to put their heart and soul into an effort to stop inflation. Why should they, when inflation is the secret of their success? They're not villains or conspirators. They're "Friends of Paper Money." There have always been "Friends of Paper Money," and they really cannot be blamed for doing anything wrong or evil.

"*It is historically true that no order of society ever perishes save by its own hand.*"

—John Maynard Keynes,
The Economic Consequences of The Peace, 1920

2
THE ONLY CAUSE OF INFLATION

There is only one cause of inflation. There can only be one cause of inflation. That cause is *artificial money*. Artificial money gets its value from what it *represents*. Real money gets its value from what it *is*, from its rarity, utility, uniformity, and durability.

In a closed society artificial money is highly acceptable. Polynesian tribesmen have used shells, beads, and stones in the same way gamblers in the casinos of Las Vegas use plastic poker chips: they're fine within their specific circle, but when a gambler and a Polynesian do business together, the Polynesian won't take poker chips and the gambler will have no use for shells, beads, and stones. Something more "universal" will have to be used as their medium of exchange.

The universal medium of exchange between differing tribal systems since 3600 B.C. has been gold or gold and silver. I saw a recent piece of economic research showing that 99.6 per cent of the people on this planet esteem gold higher than anything else as a medium of exchange. International commerce has never been possible without gold and silver and never will be.

How gold and silver gets into the monetary system of countries is best expressed in the United States Coinage Act of 1792, which is still in effect today:

> SECTION 14. *And be it further enacted,* That it shall be lawful for any person or persons[1] to bring to the mint gold and silver bullion, in order to their being coined; and that the bullion so brought shall be there assayed and coined as speedily as may be after the receipt thereof, and that free of expense to the person or persons by whom the same shall have been brought. And as soon as the said bullion shall have been coined, the person or persons by whom the same shall have been delivered, shall upon demand receive in lieu thereof coins of the same species of bullion which shall have been so delivered, weight for weight, of the pure gold or pure silver therein contained: *Provided nevertheless,* That it shall be at the mutual option of the party or parties bringing such bullion, and of the director of the said mint, to make an immediate exchange of coins for standard bullion, with a deduction of one half per cent. from the weight of the pure gold, or pure silver contained in said bullion, as an indemnification to the mint for the time which will necessarily be required for coining the said bullion, and for the advance which shall have been so made in coins.

Artificial money is introduced into gold-and-silver systems as bills of credit, certificates, notes, or I.O.U.s. Artificial money explains its usefulness this way: "Why lug around all that gold and silver? Why not let your government or your bank keep your gold and silver for you, and in return we'll issue you these lovely paper certificates which are much easier to transport? Of course it goes without saying that if you ever want your gold and silver back, all you need do is present the paper and we'll return your money to you."

Imagine the temptation of having a vault full of the people's gold and silver while the people are perfectly happy to use paper! At some point, any thinking custodian is going to say, "No one is asking for his gold and silver to be redeemed. Everyone considers paper to be money now. Paper is easier to print than gold is to dig out of the mine. Hmmmm. By printing up paper notes, I can actually *make* money!"

---

1. Of course, "person" means individual or corporation, such as a mining company.

And so, gradually, you print up more bills of credit than there is gold and silver to back them. A few people notice that certain items are more expensive this year than last, but that could be due to demand for the items, or a shortage. No big worry. Nobody complains, except a few prophets of doom who can be written off as crackpots.

You grow delirious with joy as time passes. You buy a beautiful 10-acre lot and build a mansion on it, paying with paper you printed that everyone's delighted to accept. How can you help but feel confident and somewhat self-important? This is the life! You throw a lot of cocktail parties.

Within a few years, there is so much paper in circulation that gold and silver can now be denounced as old-fashioned: who uses it anymore? People find gold and silver money in coin shops and it's way overpriced. Relics of the past. (It's interesting to note that gold and silver coin are routinely called "relics of the past" by friends of artificial money, and have been so called since . . . well, the *remotest* past).

To explain rising prices and sudden layoffs, complicated formulae appear from "institutes of economic studies," formulae that attempt to build a "value index" according to "national energy" and the "gross national product." These formulae are understood only by their creators, and each institute has a set of creators who feel their formulae are superior to others. Doctorate degrees and lofty distinctions are accorded these people, and they write textbooks that train younger minds. You give a big grant to one of these institutes for further studies and in the bargain get a nice tax deduction.

Loss of the currency's purchasing power is called "the rising cost of living" rather than "embezzlement." (What does an embezzler do but increase his victim's cost of living?)

As individual fortunes dwindle and the people clamor for relief and leadership, government and civilian spokesmen condemn "government spending" as the chief cause of inflation. ("Government," as much a creature of the ideasphere as "Uncle Sam," makes an ideal whipping boy because it can be whipped indefinitely and not break or die. In fact, as the past 15 years testify, the more government is whipped, the more brutishly powerful it grows.)

Constitutional amendments that would limit federal spending are proposed and there is much verbiage and correspondence on this. Relief and leadership are just over the horizon, the people are led to believe. As you crank out more paper, you ask the people to have a little hope and faith, and while they're at it, cut way back on their simplest pleasures. *Sacrifice*, and rest assured that our most distinguished economists are working overtime with government to try to hammer out a solution to this most pressing, most intricate problem.

What our most brilliant economists and articulate statesmen neglect to bring up is that the solution to inflation is already clearly contained in the United States Constitution.

Yes, it's right there, just waiting to be acted upon.

What you won't hear on radio or TV (surely you know how the banks and government regulations make the media walk a thin line of fear) is that YOU, personally, YOU have more power than your senators, your representatives, your state officials, even more power than the President of the United States when it comes to restoring economic well-being to your country. And you can do it IMMEDIATELY, whenever you get ready to.

You won't have to send the first telegram to your congressman. You won't have to march in protest. You won't even have to organize. There'll be no long wait for a Supreme Court decision. The "right candidate" won't have to get elected. You won't really have to do anything, in fact, except *decline* to break a law. So you have nothing to risk, either. Whoever got into trouble for declining to break a law?

To use your power, you'll need to know a little about where American money comes from. And where your power comes from. And, of course, you'll need to know about the law you're going to decline to break. Some people get fidgety when "law" is brought up in a discussion of social action, so perhaps you'd enjoy being reassured that your power is well-insulated, that you won't get into any trouble when you wield it.

We'll start, then, with the reassurance.

*"We hold these Truths to be self-evident, that all Men are created equal, that they are endowed by their Creator with certain unalienable Rights, that among these are Life, Liberty, and the Pursuit of Happiness—That to secure these Rights, Governments are instituted among Men, deriving their just Powers from the Consent of the Governed, that **whenever any Form of Government becomes destructive of these Ends, it is the Right of the People to alter or to abolish it** . . ."*

—A DECLARATION By the
REPRESENTATIVES of the
UNITED STATES OF
AMERICA,
In GENERAL CONGRESS
Assembled, July 4, 1776

3
THE RIGHT TO ALTER AND ABOLISH

Knowledgeable lawyers tell me that there is no finer state constitution than Tennessee's. The very first article in our state's Constitution is a Declaration of Rights, which means that the authors put the people first, above all else. The first section of Article I puts both state and local government firmly under the control of you and me:

> All power is inherent in the people, and all free governments are founded on their authority, and instituted for their peace, safety, and happiness.

This is certainly a comforting statement and describes the relationship of the people to government, but what if the government gradually were to begin *limiting* the peace, safety, and happiness of the people? Is there something the people can do in that case? Yes. The very next clause in Article I Section 1 spells it out in no uncertain terms:

> For the advancement of those ends, they have, at all times, an unalienable and indefeasible right to alter, reform, or abolish the government in such manner as they may think proper.

Now, if you know of a stronger guarantee of human liberty than those words, please show it to me. Not even the United States Constitution assures the individual such awesome power with such bold expression. "In such manner as they may think proper" preserves the right to *revolt in violence* if you think it proper, it even allows you to be *wrong* in the manner you choose to reform, abolish or alter the government.

Happily, the lawful remedy for economic disaster presented here does not call for violence. But it does call for a slight alteration in state governmental practice. Does knowing that your Constitution immunizes you from punishment for altering your government, does knowing this allay any fears you might have had that you could get into trouble for flexing your power in the face of officials? It sure did for me, and I hope it does for you. (If you're not a Tennessean, your state constitution assures you the implied right to alter your government lawfully, for reasons you'll soon discover. See Appendix for states with "alter and abolish" guarantee.)

There's even further insulation against trouble. In the Tennessee Constitution (and all state constitutions) there is a requirement that all officials authorized by the Constitution—all elected or appointed persons, state and local—"take an oath to support the Constitution of this State, and of the United States." What this means is that every judge, legislator, mayor, commissioner, agent, clerk, governor, law officer, sheriff—everyone of authority in state and local government must swear to support the people's "unalienable and indefeasible right to alter, reform, or abolish the government in such manner as they may think proper." **Not only must they *allow* you to reform, alter, or abolish, they must also *support* you!**

Did you know you had so much power over those smart, influential dignitaries you read about in the papers and see on TV? Perhaps you should pause a moment and let it all sink in: all government officials are your servants, and if you think they are not doing their job well, you can deal with them in such manner (humane, of course) as you may think proper. *Guaranteed by law.*

Public servants, of course, know of the power you reserve over them before they take their oath. If the terms frighten them, they can always find work elsewhere. Certainly no one forces any civilian to join government. They're there of their own free will. Their awareness of your power explains why so many state and local government employees are so congenial and cooperative. They are aware that at the slightest provocation you can arise with your awesome and *utterly lawful* power and humiliate them. You can put them out of a job if they in any way abridge your "peace, safety, and happiness."

It requires genuine dedication and unselfishness to be a good public servant, and I'm happy to say that most of my friends in government fit that description perfectly.

*"It is apparent from the whole context of the Constitution as well as the history of the times which gave birth to it, that it was the **purpose of the Convention to establish a currency consisting of the precious metals**. These were adopted by a **permanent rule** excluding the use of a perishable medium of exchange, such as of certain agricultural commodities recognized by the statutes of some States as tender for debts, or the **still more pernicious expedient of paper currency.**"*

—Andrew Jackson, 8th Annual Message to Congress, December 5, 1836

4
"A FAVOURABLE CRISIS FOR CRUSHING PAPER MONEY"

Virtually all social crises are caused and cured by money. The Constitution of the United States, which is the Supreme Law of the Land, was drafted in order to relieve the country of what George Washington dismally reported was "anarchy and confusion." This anarchy and confusion was brought about by the people's inability to produce, buy, sell, and work for units of money with value that could be counted on. The money had no substance. You would agree to produce a chair for a man at a price, but by the time you finished and got paid, the money you received would not be worth half what it was worth when you began. Therefore, people would not agree to assist one another. Bad contracts. Bickering. Bad feelings. Suspicion. Commercial paralysis.

Was George Washington less affected by inflation than you and I? The definitive constitutional historian George Bancroft portrays the father of our country as an ordinary citizen harried by overdue bills—always a symptom of paper money's disease:

> In 1786, "his income, uncertain in its amount, was not sufficient to meet his unavoidable expenses, and he became more straitened

for money than he had ever been since his boyhood; so that he was even obliged to delay paying the annual bill of his physician, to put off the tax-gatherer once and again, and, what was harder, to defer his charities . . ."[1]

Nine months before the Constitution was signed in Philadelphia, Washington wrote to General Knox: "Good God! who could have foreseen, or predicted the disorders which have arisen in these states!" We could very well be saying those same words ourselves today, you and I and our most astute statesmen, businessmen and judicial officers, because (to repeat) *inflation can't be appreciated for what it is until it's felt, until it happens*.

I remember people telling me in 1969 "We're going to have a horrible inflation where a loaf of bread will cost a dollar," and I remember answering "So what? If prices go higher, government will simply print more money. No problem."

What I was pathetically ignorant of was that when bread goes from a dime to a dollar a loaf, the entire order of things tilts on its axis: government and education fatten to insolence, quality and pride of craft vanish, drug highs are celebrated in entertainments designed for families, sexual aberrations become politicized into badges of dignity, audiences delight in blood gushing from stage and screen, pornographers open shops in neighborhoods, and—all across the land—an array of broken homes, broken oaths, broken laws, broken hearts, broken bodies.

A decade ago I could say "So what?" to inflation simply because I hadn't *felt* it. Inflation as a future thing is utterly incomprehensible. *"Who could have foreseen or predicted the disorders which have arisen. . . ."* It's precisely because we couldn't foresee ("fore*feel*"?) its disorders that we let inflation happen to us. George Washington and the Continental Congress let it happen to them for the same reason.

The permanent antidote to inflation was arrived at in the

---

1. Bancroft: *History of the United States of America*, Volume VI, New York: D. Appleton and Company, 1886, p. 179.

Constitutional Convention in Philadelphia.

At the drafting of the U.S. Constitution,[1] there were many Friends of Paper Money present. On August 16, 1787, when the discussion arose on Article I Section 8, the proposed wording was this:

> "The Legislature of the United States shall have the power to . . . coin money . . . and emit bills on the credit of the United States."[2]

A hot argument ensued on the power to emit bills of credit, which is another way of saying "printing paper money." Here are the actual words James Madison wrote describing the debate in his diary:

> Mr. G. Morris moved to strike out "and emit bills of credit." If the United States had credit such bills would be unnecessary; if they had not, unjust and useless.
>
> MADISON: Will it not be sufficient to prohibit the making them a *tender*? This will remove the temptation to emit them with unjust views. And promissory notes in that shape may in some emergencies be best.
>
> MORRIS: Striking out the words will leave room still for notes of a *responsible* minister which will do all the good without the mischief. The Monied interest will oppose the plan of Government, if paper emissions be not prohibited.
>
> COL. MASON: Though he had a mortal hatred to paper money, yet as he could not foresee all emergencies, he was unwilling to tie the hands of the Legislature. [Legislature = Congress]
>
> MR. MERCER: (A friend to paper money) It was impolitic . . . to excite the opposition of all those who were friends to paper money.
>
> MR. ELSEWORTH thought this was a favorable moment to shut and bar the door against paper money. The mischiefs of the various experiments which had been made, were now fresh in the public mind and had excited the disgust of all the respectable part of America. By withholding the power from the new Government more friends of influence would be gained to it than by almost anything else . . . Give the Government credit, and other re-

---

1. The Constitution: See APPENDIX, page 118.

2. This and all following transcript of the Constitutional Convention: James Madison, *Notes of Debates in the Federal Convention of 1787*, Ohio University Press, Athens, Ohio, 1966.

sources will offer. The power may do harm, never good.

MR. WILSON: It will have a most salutary influence on the credit of the U. States to remove the possibility of paper money. This expedient can never succeed whilst its mischiefs are remembered, and as long as it can be resorted to, it will be a bar to other resources.

MR. READ, thought the words, if not struck out, would be as alarming as the mark of the Beast in Revelation.

MR. LANGDON had rather reject the whole plan than retain the three words "and emit bills."

—*The motion for striking out carried.*

George Bancroft writes:

James Madison left his testimony that 'the pretext for a paper currency, and particularly for making the bills a tender, either for public or private debts, was cut off.' This is the interpretation of the clause, made at the time of its adoption alike by its authors and by its opponents, accepted by all the statesmen of that age, not open to dispute because too clear for argument, and never disputed so long as any one man who took part in framing the constitution remained alive.[1]

Thus, as inflation gnawed painfully on their fortunes, our forefathers deliberately and conclusively forbade Congress the power to emit bills of credit, empowering Congress only to *coin money and regulate its value*.

The door to paper money was shut but not locked. For, although Congress was not given the power to print money, it was not *denied* the power to *borrow* money. Thus, the possibility still remained that Congress' *creditor*, its *banker*, might lend Congress money and circulate the I.O.U.s of Congress as currency. Congress would not be emitting bills of credit, its bank would.

On August 28, Article I Section 10 was debated. The standing version was worded this way:

"No state shall coin money; nor grant letters of marque and reprisal; nor enter into any Treaty, alliance, or confederation; nor grant any title of Nobility."

---

1. Bancroft, *op. cit.*, p. 303.

The remarks on Article I Section 10 were short and sweet. Here is Madison's account of them:

> MR. WILSON & MR. SHERMAN moved to insert after the words "coin money" the words "nor emit bills of credit, nor make any thing but gold and silver coin a tender in payment of debts" making these prohibitions absolute, instead of making the measures allowable with the consent of the Legislature of the U.S.
>
> MR. SHERMAN thought this a favourable crisis for crushing paper money. If the consent of the Legislature could authorize emissions of it, the friends of paper money would make every exertion to get into the Legislature in order to licence it.

Mr. Wilson's and Sherman's motion was quickly agreed to and became the Supreme Law of the Land. Is there any doubt that Article I Section 10 *absolutely prohibited paper money*, crushing it forever, locking the door in its face? The system was, and is, simply ingenious. *With Section 8, Congress was denied the power to print money. But in order to keep the "friends of paper money" from obtaining the "licence" to monetize United States debt, Section 10 prohibited the states from declaring irredeemable paper (or anything other than gold and silver coin) to be a tender in payment of debts.* If you don't quite understand the foregoing sentences, and the following one as well, read and re-read them until you do; they're the most important ones in this book.

Article I Section 10's most salient part is this:

NO STATE SHALL MAKE ANY THING BUT GOLD AND SILVER COIN A TENDER IN PAYMENT OF DEBTS.

Contemporary verbal sketches of Roger Sherman, the delegate from Connecticut who was the author of those monumental 17 words, depict him as a learned man, steeped in historical knowledge but immensely bashful due to stammering speech and a physical awkwardness. He was born in 1721 in Massachusetts and learned farming and shoemaking from his father. His formal education consisted of just a few years in his youth; he filled out the rest independently. He published almanacs based on his own astronomical calculations, and included both original and classical poetry. He operated his own general store. At the age of 31 he wrote a searing indictment of paper money, *A Caveat Against Injustice: or, an Enquiry Into the Evil Consequences of a Fluctuating Medium of Exchange.* In 1766, at the age of 45, Roger Sherman was elected Judge of the Superior Court in New Haven, Connecticut, serving that office with distinction until 1788.

He was the only American to sign all four historic documents: the Continental Association of 1774, the Declaration of Independence, the Articles of Confederation, and the United States Constitution. Renowned for his high intelligence and unswerving honesty, Roger Sherman was described by John Adams "as honest as an angel and as firm in the cause of American independence as Mount Atlas."

In 1791 he was elected to the U.S. Senate where he served until his death in 1793. This quiet, humble, awkward man who farmed, educated himself, worked with his hands and his mind making shoes and poetry, making astronomical and economic calculations, making law and justice, is completely unknown to all but a handful of early American historians. Yet, if Judge Sherman hadn't stood up that hot August afternoon in Philadelphia and uttered Article I Section 10, America would have been an endless series of banana republics, regime after regime printing itself out of existence.

Thank God we're rediscovering those 17 words at this late date, hopefully in time to avert the tragedy that is sure to envelop us if we should choose to remain blind to them.

Those 17 words are the American Reality.

Thomas Jefferson paid Judge Sherman the most severe and valuable compliment: "Roger Sherman was a man who never said a foolish thing in his life."

Let's have 60 seconds of silent prayer for the good deed of *Roger Sherman*

"I place economy among the first and most important virtues and public debt as the greatest of dangers to be feared . . . We must not let our rulers load us with perpetual debt. We must make our choice between economy and liberty or profusion and servitude . . . The same prudence which in private life would forbid our paying money for unexplained projects, forbids it in the disposition of public money. We are endeavoring to reduce the government to the practice of rigid economy to avoid burdening the people . . ."

—Thomas Jefferson

5
A SUDDEN SENSE OF PROSPERITY AND TRANQUILLITY

It took a little more than four months to write the U.S. Constitution, and almost a year for the states to ratify it. Then another year for the government to be set up. The most immediate relief brought about by the Constitution was economic. The cause of this economic relief was Article I Section 10, which prohibited the states from enforcing payment in anything but gold and silver coin. If people wanted to, they could make deals using for exchange cattle, paper money, real estate, tobacco, chickens, peanuts — *anything* they could agree on. But when it came to the state's participation in anyone's economic life, such as enforcing fines, taxes, judgments, etc., the terms were spelled out quite clearly and absolutely in Article I Section 10. Nothing but gold and silver coin. NO THING.

Did putting America on a sound money basis hurt anyone? Did it cause a disastrous economic upheaval? Did it throw bankers into bankruptcy, businessmen out of business, government employees out into the cold? The best source of information on this should be none other than George Washington, who was a businessman, bureaucrat, farmer, banker, legislator, and military man, among other things. This excerpt is from a letter he wrote to his good friend, the Marquis de LaFayette, dated June 3, 1790, less than a year after the ratification of the Constitution. It shows quite dramatically what happens when an economy goes from paper money to gold and silver coin:

> You have doubtless been informed, from time to time, of the happy progress of our affairs. The principal difficulties seem in a great measure to have been surmounted. Our revenues have been *considerably more productive than it was imagined they would be*. I mention this to show the *spirit of enterprise* that prevails.

How about that! Revenues "more productive than it was imagined they would be." Couldn't we use some "considerably more productive revenues" and some "spirit of enterprise" these days? All it takes is gold and silver coin.

The public record is filled with jubilant reports of the effects of the Constitution's monetary system. The December 16, 1789 edition of the *The Pennsylvania Gazette* exclaimed:

> Since the federal constitution has removed all danger of our having a paper tender, our trade is advanced fifty percent. Our monied people can trust their cash abroad[1], and have brought their coin into circulation.

Again Washington wrote to LaFayette. It's March 19, 1791:

> Our country, my dear sir, is fast progressing in its political importance and social happiness.

On July 19, 1791, in a letter to Catherine Macaulay Graham, Washington wrote:

> The United States enjoys a sense of prosperity and tranquillity under the new government that could hardly have been hoped for.

And finally, on July 20, 1791, Washington wrote with

---

1. The word "abroad" here means "in circulation." Before Article I Section 10, the government had been reneging on its promise to redeem its obligations in gold or silver. Rather than spend this paper currency at a fraction of its face value, many people saved it in the expectation that it would someday be redeemable at par. Their patience was rewarded, for the Constitution established a government that could be *trusted*.

glowing exuberance to David Humphreys:

> Tranquillity reigns among the people with that disposition towards the general government which is likely to preserve it. Our public credit stands on that high ground which three years ago it would have been considered as a species of madness to have foretold.

In other words, Washington was saying "If anyone had predicted that our economic and societal problems could have been solved by simply making nothing but gold and silver coin our money, he would have been called crazy."

Like so many people today, Washington had originally felt that the "anarchy and confusion" was being caused by a great host of demons, paper money being just one of them. What he didn't realize until after the ratification was that irredeemable paper money had been the *sole creator* of those demons. When *it* vanished, the *demons* vanished.

Since paper money requires no labor to exist, it rewards people who perform no labor. Non-working people who receive rewards have an exaggerated sense of their worth. "Non-work" includes vacuum work. "Vacuum-work" is work performed in an area there's no real demand for, like dumb projects (Jefferson called them "unexplained projects"). Government rewards vacuum-work highly, either directly or through tax advantages to persons who subsidize vacuum-work.

When non-working people receive rewards for non-work, it turns working people against their own jobs. Reward for non-work makes working people consider the advantages of not working. Non-work is a failure to demonstrate one's capabilities as a human being. Since non-work is a statement that one is not willing directly to assist humanity, you can be sure that the rewards from non-work will be spent on things that belittle and harm humanity. Instead of contributing to humanity, the rewarded non-worker commits himself to the source of his reward, that incorporation of humanity called government.

With such allegiance from rewarded non-workers and

workers doing things for which there is no real demand, a government elected by the people can construct an entire block of non-workers and vacuum-workers *to grant it unlimited power over real workers*. A rewarded non-worker is a self-declared enemy of his fellow man, conspiring with his government to create chaos, bloodshed, injustice, corruption, hardship, and heartbreak. It was so in Washington's day and it is so in ours. It's always been so.

Inflation turns people into weightless balloons, all hollow inside. The solid substance has been removed. We "float," just like our money. Our skins are blown all out of proportion, and we have nothing to offer but appearance. Appearance and hype are everything, just like the money. Our inner selves are just air. Our outer selves are what we *are*: shells, skins. This must have been the condition T.S. Eliot was describing with his image of "hollow men." In every inflation that has ever occurred, the people develop an obsession for external things: sports, violence, pornography, and especially fashion and gesture. These are the ornaments of tyranny.

No historian can show you a tyranny founded on a free-flowing money base of gold and silver coin, *because tyranny and economic freedom are opposites*. Conversely, *every* tyranny in history has resulted from the debasement (de-*base* = removing the basic value) of the people's gold and silver money.

With a sense of forgiveness, I must mention here that the actual legislators of money debasement, in ours and other countries, are typically persons operating in good faith who simply don't know what they're doing. We allow them to debase our money because *we* don't know what *we're* doing. Remember, inflation is like pain: it can't be known until it's experienced. This is why deadly inflations are almost always spaced with a couple of generations in between.

All the horrors of the managed paper economy were snuffed out in 1789 by Article I Section 10, right before

George Washington's astonished eyes. It put non-workers to work and gave them value, infused them with "a spirit of enterprise." Painlessly, miraculously, it restored sanity and purpose to a badly shaken population. The wonderful thing about gold and silver is that it *lets you know precisely what your worth is*. It enables you to plan ahead, to feel proud of yourself and your work. Bad neurotic habits just break themselves when you know how valuable you are.

Gold and silver stops politicians from creating floods of money to spend on programs that encourage non- and vacuum-work, it stops banks from creating loans out of thin air to underwrite dumb projects, it . . . here I am in the middle of a sales pitch. Why should I be selling you on gold and silver coin? Why should I ask *anyone* to please let's start using gold and silver coin for money? Begging people to return to a gold and silver monetary base in the United States of America is as stupid as begging Congress to give women the right to vote. Women already have the right to vote, and WE ALREADY HAVE A GOLD AND SILVER MONETARY BASE IN THE UNITED STATES! Judge Roger Sherman, God bless his soul, saw to that on August 28, 1787, in a law that has never been repealed, rescinded, or amended in any way whatsoever!

NO STATE SHALL MAKE ANY THING BUT GOLD AND SILVER COIN A TENDER IN PAYMENT OF DEBTS.

If we already have a gold and silver monetary base, why then do we not have gold and silver coinage in circulation? What has happened to the law? Are we being governed by a bunch of criminals?

"*Those who create and issue money and credit direct the policies of government and hold in the hollow of their hands the destiny of the people.*"

—Rt. Hon. Reginald McKenna,
Midland Bank of England,
Secretary of the Exchequer, 1920

"*In the United States today we have in effect two governments . . . We have the duly constituted Government . . . Then we have an independent, uncontrolled and uncoordinated government in the Federal Reserve System, operating the money powers which are reserved to Congress by the Constitution.*"

—Congressman Wright Patman,
Chairman, House Banking Committee

"*A pro-International Monetary Fund Seminar of eminent economists couldn't agree on what 'money' is or how banks create it.*"

—The Wall Street Journal
September 24, 1971

6
WEAVERS OF "THE AMERICAN DREAM": THE FRIENDS OF PAPER MONEY

It's a matter of history that in 1913, the Friends of Paper Money gained a real stronghold on the American economic system through the Federal Reserve Act. In the passage of that Act, a small group of world bankers with a long and carefully-guarded, *very* private history of manipulating the affairs of rulers "got into the Legislature," just as Roger Sherman feared they would, and obtained "licence" to print money.

There's nothing in the Constitution to prevent Congress from contracting with a private corporation for the management of a popular currency. *The Federal Reserve, a private corporation?* Yes. Super-private. Its voting stockholders are kept in secret; they're known to no one, not even the President of the United States. The Federal Reserve System is not part of the U.S. Government, and has never been audited by the General Accounting Office or any government agency. Of course, it *seems* to be an official department, with the President appointing some directors and such, but the Federal Reserve is completely autonomous. Asked "Do you approve of the latest credit-tightening moves?" Treasury Secretary David M. Kennedy answered in *U.S. News & World Report* May 5, 1969, "It's not my job to approve or disapprove. It is the action of the Federal Reserve."

The chief architect of the Federal Reserve System was a world banker of extraordinary ability, Paul Moritz Warburg, who had come to this country from Germany in 1902. He was born a rich baby, an heir to the powerful Frankfurt banking house of M. N. Warburg & Company. Reading Paul Warburg's speeches on money feels like dipping your hand into a bucket of diamonds: his words are winningly precise, hard, correct. I admire him without reservation. It would take nothing less than a man of Mr. Warburg's brilliance to sell the concept of central banking to the discerning American people. Here's a sample of his salesmanship, from an address he gave at Columbia University in 1907:

> In order to conserve the interests of the public, banks should be permitted, within certain limitations with respect to capital, to issue circulating notes. They should be redeemable (for gold and silver coin) over a bank's counter, at the United States Treasury, and at convenient points throughout the country, thereby maintaining the notes at par throughout the country.
>
> While I believe that such a currency can be successfully applied to the sixty-five hundred banks now in existence, yet judged from an historical and scientific standpoint, the currency system of a country can best be administered through the instrumentality of a central bank of issue.
>
> With a pronounced trend in favor of centralization, with the popular and growing demand that all corporations, national in their scope and character, be regulated by the national government, is it not logical and fair to assume that public sentiment will presently demand that the government's receipts and disbursements shall be made through a central bank?[1]

If I'd been present at that lecture, I probably would have cheered Mr. Warburg on. His words plainly make sense. Who could have foreseen that between 1923 and 1929, the Federal Reserve would print up a *62 per cent inflation* and then suddenly stop, whiplashing the country into the crash of '29, followed by a numbing depression that lasted

---

1. *The Currency Problem*, Columbia University Press, 1908, p. 50 ff.

more than a decade? Who could have foreseen all the stops and starts which have plagued our economy since the creation of the Federal Reserve? Who could have predicted the wars, the hardships, the moral decay, the internal division? Who could have predicted that the national debt would have risen from one billion dollars in 1913 to *trillions* in the 1980's? And who pays off that debt? You and your kids.

Well, is the Federal Reserve a giant, sinister conspiracy out to destroy and/or enslave us, a menacing foe against which we are powerless? Of course not. Federal Reserve people are nice folks, good members of their communities. They go to church, play golf, contribute to worthwhile charities just as you may do. And like most people in business, they have a product to sell. To sell this product, they have to overcome customer resistance.

Like McDonald's or "The 10 O'Clock News" or Coca-Cola or the Avon lady, the Federal Reserve operates by *staking a claim on your imagination*. They've done everything within the law to get you to believe in their product. The Federal Reserve exists because you *let it* exist. You patronize its nationwide franchises, the friendly banks opening onto Main Street. You believe in the Federal Reserve just as you believe in Coca-Cola and your insurance man, and that's why irredeemable paper notes have become the money you use, the money you're finding ever more difficult to keep track of.

Since the Federal Reserve, like a dream, exists because you believe in it, it can cease to exist as soon as you stop believing in it. That's the way the ideasphere works. The 10 O'Clock News surrenders its claim on you the instant you turn off your TV. Moreover, most of the people at the top of the Federal Reserve *know* that they owe their livelihood to your credence in them, and that once you decide that their product is not what it's cracked up to be, you can make them improve it. (In passing, isn't it strange how silent Ralph Nader is about our faulty Federal Reserve money?)

But as long as you are willing to reduce your circumstances in order to make room for greater floods of paper and digital "money supply," the people at the Federal Reserve and their member banks *really see no need to improve their product.*

As long as you're willing to believe that the cause of inflation is government spending or OPEC oil or the "Crisis in Iran" or wherever, as long as you're willing to get out and politick for the candidate whom you think will stop inflation (has any candidate *ever* licked inflation upon election?), as long as you think the President's "Inflation Fighter" (usually a Federal Reserve director or governor or intimate) can lick inflation, as long as you're willing to gripe and complain and bicker with your grocer and the power companies and your gas-pumper about what they're charging you, *as long as you're content to howl at the moon* . . . the Friends of Paper Money have no reason to lift a finger to change things.

Except to raise interest rates, which penalizes you more and enables them to increase their grasp on your pursestrings several notches while you're trying to figure out why you got laid off.

"... He has combined with others to subject us to a Jurisdiction foreign to our Constitution, and unacknowledged by our Laws...."

—A DECLARATION By the REPRESENTATIVES of the UNITED STATES OF AMERICA, In GENERAL CONGRESS Assembled, July 4, 1776

"An inefficient, unemployed, disorganized Europe is an extant example of how much man can suffer and how far society can decay.

"Economic privation proceeds by easy stages, and so long as men suffer it patiently the outside world cares little. Physical efficiency and resistance to disease slowly diminish, but life proceeds somehow, until the limit of human endurance is reached at last and counsels of despair and madness stir the sufferers from the lethargy which precedes the crisis. Then man shakes himself and the bonds of custom are loosed. The power of ideas is sovereign, and he listens to whatever instruction of hope, illusion, or revenge is carried to him on the air."

—John Maynard Keynes,
The Economic Consequences of The Peace, 1920

7
BROTHER MAX

Across the Atlantic, the German federal reserve—a central bank of issue called the *Reichsbank*—performed an experiment in artificial money that devastated the German people, 1916-1923. Pearl S. Buck wrote a book about it with Erna von Pustau called *How It Happens* (New York: The John Day Company, 1947). Genocide by paper flood is documented in this book with dramatic eye-witness vividness.

In the beginning days, as the *Reichsbank* started issuing paper credit out of thin air, the German press excitedly called inflation "the miracle of German industry!" No wonder. Everybody had money and credit, just like in America in the go-go 1960's. But soon the dream turned nightmarish. Recalling her brother's remarks about his normally thrifty wife, Frau von Pustau describes Germany around 1919:

> "Robert first looked puzzled, then he said to me, 'You know, Hilde is just how women ought to be. *But it's madness to save* nowadays.' Saving is the very source of wealth and health of a sound nation. We were on our way to becoming a crazy, a neurotic, a mad nation."

The press cooperated not with the struggling, suffering

people who looked to their newspapers for answers, but with the Friends of Paper Money. No attempt was made to publish or broadcast the one true cause of inflation, to lead the people to the solution. Unfortunately for them, the Germans had had no Roger Sherman, no Article I Section 10; they were completely at the mercy of the *Reichsbank* and industry (itself indebted to the *Reichsbank*) and, of course, the government (the *Reichsbank's* largest debtor). Please note that the Director of the *Reichsbank* at this time was none other than Max Warburg, the brother of Paul, who created and served as a governor of America's Federal Reserve Board. Also note that during much of this period, our boys and German boys were fighting the bloodiest war in world history, up to then. Millions of people got killed.

The newspapers and radios published all kinds of tips and hints on how to live with inflation, buying cheaper cuts of meat, staying cold in winter, just generally reducing one's needs in the interests of "conservation"—that kind of thing, with which you're quite familiar.

"Inflation is a thing which has slipped out of control of everyone," the newspapers lamented; as times grew worse, the media began blaming "foreigners," gold speculators, and gold hoarders. Of course, hoarding gold is just about the only defense anyone has against inflation. Even in the last frantic days, the press was still terming inflation "a catastrophe of nature." Do you see any similarities between the media then and now?

Frau von Pustau says:

> By the end of the year my allowance and all the money I earned were not worth one cup of coffee. You could go to the baker in the morning and buy two rolls for 20 marks; but go there in the afternoon, and the same two rolls were 25 marks. The baker didn't know how it happened. His customers didn't know how it happened. It had somehow to do with the dollar, somehow to do with the stock exchange—and somehow, maybe, to do with the Jews.

Confusion, mass ignorance, debates flaming from all sides, complicated solutions proposed by experts: "All these technical questions made it difficult for anybody to understand for a long time what was happening," Frau von Pustau says. And while no one was understanding, the Friends of Paper Money were pocketing more and more of the people's property.

She recalls:

> When Father came back from vacation, he said that the workers had discovered the 'trick of inflation,' which was to figure the value of money in gold. Time and again, the workers struck for the 'adjustment of their wages,' paid daily in exact accordance with the daily mark devaluation.

Those who quickly converted to gold were able to survive the inflation with their resources reasonably intact. **"Quickly converting to gold" is but one step below having a redeemable currency.** For those who remained ignorant of the "trick of inflation," says Frau von Pustau, "life was madness, nightmare, desperation, chaos."

Finally, out of the chaos came the cure. But the cure became a political game, a long, drawn out affair that lasted nearly six months as the various factions in government and business jockeyed for position to see who would be given credit for bringing about the cure. Says Frau von Pustau:

> The government struggled hard to restore the gold standard. But the Minister of Finance was the socialist Hilferding. Big business was ready, now, to restore the gold standard; but the whole clique, including the agriculture, peasants, and Junkers wanted to be given credit for restoring sound and solid money. While this struggle went on, chaos increased.

And prostitution and suicide and every kind of street crime imaginable. Even *unimaginable*: it got so bad, according to Frau von Pustau, that chunks of meat were butchered from the flanks of horses standing at rest in front of their wagons and were either sold or eaten on the spot.

At length, with a loaf of bread costing billions of marks, the currency was made redeemable in gold coin and instantly the stormy sea calmed. But enormous damage had been done, both past and future. For the "honor" of restoring a sound mark was given to Dr. Hjalmar Schacht, who was skyrocketed by the media to national heroism, fame and adulation because of his "accomplishment." Because he had "rescued Germany," anyone Dr. Schacht associated with would be accorded great public esteem. It's history that Hjalmar Schacht chose to associate himself with Adolf Hitler, becoming the Fuhrer's chief economic advisor.

In 1949, China was drowned in an inflation identical to the German one, resulting in Mao Tse Tung's repressive dictatorship. In 1946, the Hungarian government's central bank printed the 10-quintrillion Pengo note which, before the Second World War, would have bought the whole country; in April 1946, a 10-quintrillion Pengo couldn't purchase a dozen eggs. With the collapse of the Hungarian economy, of course, came communist dictatorship. And so on, globally.

A giant step toward an American 10-quintrillion dollar note was taken with the passage last March of "The Depository Institutions Deregulation and Monetary Control Act of 1980." This Act empowers the Federal Reserve to declare almost *anything* to be money, and compels all banks to join its system.

Truly, as Frédéric Bastiat wrote in the last century, "Often the masses are plundered and do not know it."

"*The* same monetary system that was established on April 2, 1792, is ***in effect today.***"

      —Bruce A. Budlong,
       Acting Director, Special
       Financing Staff, *Department of the Treasury*, Fiscal Service

"*The* terms 'lawful money' and 'lawful money of the United States' shall be construed to mean gold or silver coin of the United States."

      —12 UNITED STATES CODE 152

"*All* coins and currencies of the United States (including Federal Reserve notes and circulating notes of Federal Reserve banks and national banking associations), regardless of when coined or issued, shall be legal tender for all debts, public and private, public charges, taxes, duties, and dues."

      —31 UNITED STATES CODE 392

8
IS DREAM MONEY **LAWFUL** MONEY?

This may surprise you, but Congress has never declared Federal Reserve notes to be a legal tender in payment of debts. Doubt me? Look at your currency: "... LEGAL TENDER FOR ALL DEBTS PUBLIC AND PRIVATE."

The word "FOR" is used rather than "IN PAYMENT OF." Was this just accidental? No. It is well-settled in the courts that lawmakers are presumed to have selected each word that makes up a statute carefully and deliberately, lest the statute be considered void for vagueness. We can be sure, then, that when Congress chose NOT to use "IN PAYMENT OF," it did so for a good reason, that good reason being the hard fact that *no debt can be paid in full in the eyes of American jurisprudence unless paid in gold or silver coined and regulated in value by Congress,* courtesy of Article I Sections 8 and 10. (See "The U.S. Monetary System," p. 148.)

About all a Federal Reserve note can legally do is wipe out one debt and replace it with *itself*, another debt, a note that promises nothing. If anything's been *paid*, the payment occurs only in the minds of the parties—in the ideasphere—not the real world.

It's important for you to mark well that Federal Reserve notes are *not your government's money.* They bear likenesses of our presidents, they bear the signatures of our Treasurer and the Secretary of the Treasury, they bear beautiful engravings of our most sacred political monuments, and even—since the late 1950's—the pious religious motto "In God We Trust," *but they are not your government's money.* So when you revile American Dream money, you're in no way insulting your government. Federal Reserve paper is not lawful money, not government money. It is the scrip of a private corporation partially owned by your local banker. Whether it's a $100 bill or a $1 bill, a Federal Reserve note is intrinsically worth about one cent. Its extrinsic worth is whatever it will buy from day to day in the marketplace, just like the 1916-1923 German mark.

Is this any kind of money for a stable country to have?

Between 1913 and 1963, the Federal Reserve promised redeemability in lawful money on their notes. But in 1963, they began issuing notes *minus* the redeemability promise. This enabled your banker to issue you a note that said "In God We Trust" in exchange for your silver dollar, without his having to exchange that silver dollar back for the note. An unfair deal, you might say, but who took steps to prevent it?

Interestingly, the first 50,000,000 no-promise Federal Reserve notes were shipped out on November 26, 1963, which happened to be the day of John F. Kennedy's funeral. A coin dealer friend of mine says, "You know, they couldn't have picked a better day to catch the people off guard." [1]

These days it looks like there's not enough gold and silver "to go around." That's because there's so much paper. Inflation always makes people think there's a shortage in precious metals. The reason is simple: *Increased paper increases prices.*

It looks, too, as though we're "off the gold standard," as a banker told me in earnest not long ago. Both this and the "not enough" assumptions are based on *pure hearsay.* How rarely we bother to check things out! How easily we sur-

---

1. See Appendix, page 143 ff.

render our lives to gossip! Oh, that ideasphere! For America to be "off the gold (or silver) standard" the Coinage Act of April 2, 1792, which specifies in detail how our money is to be made, would have to be rescinded or repealed by Congress. Then, a constitutional amendment permitting the states to make something other than gold and silver coin a tender in payment of debts would have to be passed and *ratified by three-fourths of the states*.

As of 1981, neither of these events has happened. God help us if they ever *should* happen.

It is the *Federal Reserve*'s monetary system that is no longer on the gold or silver standard. In the Federal Reserve's own published statement:

> Today, in the United States, there are only two kinds of money in use in significant amounts—currency (paper money and coins in the pockets and purses of the public) and demand deposits (checking accounts in commercial banks). Since $1 in currency and $1 in demand deposits are freely convertible into each other at the option of a bank's customer, both are money to an equal degree. What . . . makes these instruments acceptable at face value payment of all debts? Mainly, it is the *confidence* people have that they will be able to exchange such money for real goods and services whenever they choose to do so.[1]

So there you have it: **paper** and **confidence** are the monies in which we conduct our daily commercial transactions, with our friendly banker as our perpetual middleman. But have the instruments of the Federal Reserve monetary system ever qualified to be the money in which the transactions of government must be conducted? Let's investigate.

The government is limited to a special kind of money by federal statute. For, you see, in order to live up to the Constitution's promise of establishing domestic tranquillity and promoting the general welfare, the people in-

---

1. *Modern Money Mechanics*, Dorothy Nichols, published 1975 by the Federal Reserve Bank of Chicago. Available from Research Department, Federal Reserve Bank of Chicago, P.O. Box 834, Chicago, Illinois 60690.

structed their representatives to keep all official accounts and proceedings in "the money of account of the United States." First legislated in the Coinage Act of 1792, this requirement is found in current law at Section 371 of Title 31 of the United States Code, which you should *memorize:*

31 UNITED STATES CODE 371

The money of account of the United States shall be expressed in dollars or units, dimes or tenths, cents or hundredths, and mills or thousandths, a dime being the tenth part of a dollar, a cent the hundredth part of a dollar, a mill the thousandth part of a dollar; - and **all accounts in the public offices and all proceedings in the courts shall be kept and had in conformity to this regulation.**

Thus, it is federal regulation that all accounts in the public offices and all proceedings in the courts must be conducted in whatever has been declared to be "the money of account of the United States," this money being expressed—or measured—in "dollars."

A dollar, therefore, is neither a coin nor a piece of paper, but simply the name of the unit by which the value of money is measured, just as "quart" is the name of a unit by which liquid is measured. A dealer selling a car for "1500 quarts" would surely be asked "Quarts of *what?*" Where, then, is the frivolity in asking of a $15 parking ticket, "Fifteen dollars of *what?*"?

When courts and public offices require you to pay in dollars, the dollars must—by the above law—be dollars (or **units) of the money of account of the United States.** Is there any doubt in your mind as to what the money of account of the United States is?

The Coinage Act of 1792 specifically declared gold and silver to be "as money in the United States." But in 1933, Congress suspended our currency's redemption in gold, and in 1968 suspended the redemption of silver certificates in silver. (In both cases, the excuse was "temporary emergency," as it always is when governments work with bankers to harvest the people's property without due process.) The cumulative effect of those acts of 1933 and 1968 was this:

Congress eliminated the money of account of the United States from the banking system without declaring a replacement, with the astonishing result that neither our courts nor our public offices are complying with 31 U.S.C. 371!

Federal Reserve notes and all those confidence-building, important-looking instruments of Federal Reserve banking may be "money," all right, but they've never been declared to be the money of account of the United States, as gold and silver have. They may even be measured in dollars or units, but not in dollars or units of the money of account of the United States.

Federal Reserve notes can be a tender *for* debts, and they may even be "lawful" money, in the sense that they've never been specifically declared *un*lawful, but they are not the money of account of the United States that is measured in dollars in which "all accounts in the public offices and all the proceedings in the courts shall be kept and had."[1] And if you doubt me, just ask any judge or lawyer or attorney general to show you legislation that disproves me.

In short, Federal Reserve notes are compelling images charged with charm and enchantment, like movies and TV and comic strips and stereo and colorful pages in magazines. If you believe that they, or the bank demand deposits for which they are redeemable, are the money the law requires us to pay into our government, you're living in a dream world.

---

1. I'm being intentionally repetitive about this "money-of-account-of-the-United-States-that-is-expressed-in-dollars" business because there's so much misinformation we *must* set right. The dollar is NOT the money of account, it is the UNIT by which the money of account is measured. Please read and re-read this section until you have it cold.

"*All the perplexities, confusion and distress in America arise not from defects in their constitution or confederation, not from a want of honor or virtue so much as from downright ignorance of the nature of coin, credit, and circulation.*"
—John Adams to Thomas Jefferson, 1787

"*I have studied finance and economics and international trade all my life, and now, after these recent events, I have come to the conclusion that I know nothing whatever about any of them.*"
—Paul Moritz Warburg, remarking on the Crash of 1929, as quoted in *The Nation*, February 3, 1932

"*We have awakened forces that nobody is at all familiar with.*"
—John Connally, Secretary of the Treasury, quoted in *The Wall Street Journal*, August 14, 1971

9
STARTING THE MIRACLE BY REDUCING THE IGNORANCE FACTOR

Sir William Gladstone called the United States Constitution "The most wonderful work ever struck off at a given time by the brain and purpose of man." Yet, its nature and providence are unknown—according to a survey in the Bicentennial year—to over 90% of the American people. Ninety per cent of the American people are ignorant of a great many lawful guarantees of prosperity and happiness that are theirs simply for the asking. Amazing!

The ignorance factor is not limited to the people; it is shared in the realms of government as well. I have interviewed many important government officials who are almost totally unaware of their rights—or anyone else's—under the very document they are sworn to support. I have had the dubious pleasure of introducing for the first time to numerous state and local officials the prohibition in Article I Section 10 against paper money.

When an honest official discovers that he's been taking money under state authority in violation of the Constitution and his oath, he is shocked. We act strangely under shock. One typical response I hear is "Why didn't anybody tell me this? How did this happen?"

One judge told me in open court "The state must use the currency Congress issues." This statement is wrong on two counts:

>1. The Congress, by law, does not tell the States what shall be tender. The Constitution, thanks to the more knowledgeable Judge Sherman, provides that the *States* shall tell *Congress* what lawful tender shall be: nothing but gold and silver coin.
>
>2. Congress *doesn't* issue Federal Reserve notes; a nongovernmental, private "banker's bank" issues these notes.

Thus, a man with considerable power over the economic fortunes of his peers is completely ignorant of both the natural and statutory laws of money. Again, I must repeat, it's no reflection on his moral character or intelligence or even his judicial preparedness. The ignorance of money is widespread, deep. **We are *all* victims of the money blackout.** The Friends of Paper Money work as hard keeping us ignorant of money as some parents work keeping their kids believing in Santa Claus.

After the initial shock, the honest public official begins to worry in the back of his mind about all this. One told me he figured that there *must* be a law somewhere that permitted the state to make paper money a tender. Otherwise, he said, "The whole damn state's crazy." When he failed to turn up any such law after weeks of looking, he experienced profound misgivings about the whole purpose of government. He even considered resigning. He and his colleagues who were taking and giving money in the name of the state (or municipal) government were actually perjuring their Constitutional Oath! It tore at his conscience.

The whole damn state's not crazy. For, in my opinion, no one in state or local government is violating his oath of office by *accepting* paper money or by *paying* in paper money. As long as people are willing to contribute to their government (or accept from it) paper money, copper, digits, automobiles, or real estate the government is under no moral obligation to change its ways. Any law that prohibits government from accepting contributions from its citizens or discharging its debts cheaply would be a bad law indeed.

Article I Section 10 doesn't prohibit the state from accepting paper money. It merely prohibits the state from declaring that things other than gold and silver coin are lawful tender. In other words, when the state Attorney General is asked "What does the state declare is legal tender?" he *must* answer "Gold and silver coin."

If any property or sales tax form or citation—any bill from state or local government, even a parking ticket—is labelled "Dollars," you have the right to ask the state if it means dollars of the money of account of the United States, and if so, *what* is the money of account?

The state is not likely to answer that the instrument is not denominated in the money of account, nor is it likely to tell you what the money of account is. You'll be in a quandary.

Of course, there will be no state law declaring paper to be a tender in payment of debts. It would be an embarrassing, flagrant violation of the United States Constitution. Here's an example of how rigidly a state must adhere to Article I Section 10. This is a case cited in the NOTES TO DECISIONS involving Article I Section 10 as published in the Tennessee Code Annotated:

> Since nothing but gold and silver coin is a legal tender, tender in bank notes of the bank of the United States to redeem land sold under execution, *if objected to* will not be good, although equal to coin.
>
> —LOWRY v McGHEE (1835)
> 16 Tenn. 242

So there it is, still on the books in the 1980 edition, a case in which the court had no choice but to sustain a man's objection to paper currency, *even though the currency was redeemable in gold and silver coin*! You can imagine what that court would have said to irredeemable Federal Reserve paper.

If there is no law entitling the state to enforce payment in paper money, and if the state cannot tell you what the money of account of the United States is, you and the state have reached an impasse in your economic favor, or what the St. Louis monetary realist Amos Bruce calls "a Mexican standoff." You'll pay as soon as they show you how you can.

Yes, if you choose NOT to contribute paper money to your state and local government, you have the total BLESSING of the United States Constitution (and the ghost of Judge Roger Sherman, who will surely be smiling down upon you from the heavens) until paper money is made redeemable for gold and silver coin. You even have the blessing of the courts and officials of government, since they have *sworn of their own volition to support Judge Sherman's 17 words*.

And what if some government official should come after you and bug you in any way? *You* have the protection of the law, not he. All states have official misconduct statutes. Here's the one for Tennessee:

> **TENNESSEE CODE 39-3203** *Official Oppression—Penalty.*—If any person, by color of his office, willfully and corruptly oppress any person, under pretense of acting in his official capacity, he shall be punished by fine not exceeding one thousand dollars ($1,000), or imprisonment in the county jail not exceeding one (1) year.

Now, the important words in this statute are "willfully and corruptly." This means that you must first inform the official of Article I Section 10, of the fact that bank credits and Federal Reserve paper money are not gold and silver coin, and that you know he is bound by oath to support the Constitution. Explain to him that he, being part of government, is limited to taking only the money of account of the United States, and until you know what that money is, you cannot pay lawfully and properly. You see, you're helping *him* not to break the law by *educating him*. If you wanted to be especially helpful, you might send him a copy of this book. (Thank you.) Now you've given him fair warning. If he tries to oppress you from this point onward, he is being "willful and corrupt," and all you have to do—if the District Attorney plays dead—is appear before a Grand Jury yourself, tell those taxpayers what this official did, and get him *indicted!*

Don't believe the false notion that government officials are permitted to operate corruptly and safely behind "sovereign immunity" laws. There are no sovereigns in America (except you, the people), and no government official is immune from justice if he abuses your rights. You can establish a personal fortune upon the ruins of anyone who runs roughshod over your Constitutional guarantees: he who would unlawfully jeopardize *your* property loses property to you, and that's what justice is all about. Here's the law:

42 UNITED STATES CODE 1983 [1]

Civil action for deprivation of rights. Every person who, under color of any statute, ordinance, regulation, custom, or usage, of any State or Territory, subjects, or causes to be subjected, any citizen of the United States or other person within the jurisdiction thereof to the deprivation of any rights, privileges, or immunities secured by the Constitution and laws, shall be liable to the party injured in an action at law, suit in equity, or other proper proceeding for redress.

Perhaps George Bancroft's "abstract of the avowed convictions of the great statesmen and jurists who made the Constitution" will intensify the potency of Article I Section 10 in the minds of otherwise oppressive officials and eliminate any need for legal action. Show them Bancroft's words:

> History can not name a man who has gained enduring honor by causing the issue of paper money. Wherever such paper has been employed, it has in every case thrown upon its authors the burden of exculpation under the plea of pressing necessity.
>
> Paper money has no hold, and from its very nature can acquire no hold, on the conscience or affections of the people. It impairs all certainty of possession, and taxes none so heavily as the class who earn their scant possession by daily labor. It injures the husbandman by a twofold diminution of the exchangeable value of

---

1. Upheld by the Supreme Court only last year: "The innocent individual who is harmed by an abuse of governmental authority is assured that he will be compensated for his injury." **Owen vs. City of Independence,** 100 S.Ct. 1398 (1980).

his harvest. It is the favorite of those who seek gain without willingness to toil; it is the deadly foe of industry. No powerful political party ever permanently rested for support on the theory that it is wise and right. No statesman has been thought well of by his kind in a succeeding generation for having been its promoter.[1]

I have found that as soon as even the most ornery government enforcement people *figure out* what the issue is all about (and you have to help them, work with them), *they automatically join your side*. They HAVE to, because the *Constitution* is on your side. Not to agree with you is to deplore the Constitution, and many people still consider that TREASON.

---

1. Bancroft, *op. cit.*, p. 304

For a vigorous continuing education in money, receive the monthly bulletin of the Monetary Realists Society, P.O. Box 10744, St. Louis, MO 63129. Twelve issues for a costs donation of $10.

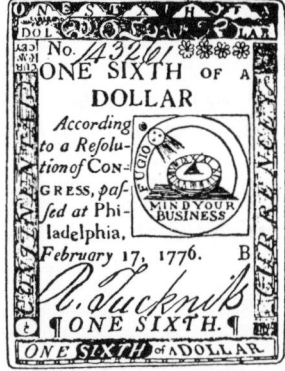

IDEASPHERE MONEY

These are examples of the money George Washington was complaining about. They are I.O.U.s containing uplifting mottoes—"*Perseverando*" ("Keep on truckin' "), "We Are One," "In God We Trust," etc.—as well as the signatures of important dignitaries. The people trusted them as long as they could be redeemed in gold and silver. It took years, though, for the situation to get so bad the people started shooting up state legislatures and rioting and pillaging. Finally, Article I Sections 8 and 10 of the Constitution solved all the problems.

George Washington wrote to John Laurens in 1781, "Experience has demonstrated the impracticability long to maintain a paper credit without funds for its redemption."

The Constitution appoints the *States* as the only guardians of those funds. But our states have been sleeping, because we have allowed them to.

"*This* constitution, and the laws made in pursuance thereof, shall be the supreme law of the land; and the judges in every state shall be bound thereby, any thing in the constitution or laws of any state to the contrary notwithstanding . . . and all officers both of the United States and of the several States shall be **bound by oath to support this constitution.**"
—ARTICLE 6, CONSTITUTION of
the UNITED STATES

"*Whoever*, having taken a lawful oath, shall affirm willfully, **corruptly and falsely touching a matter material to the point in question**, shall be guilty of perjury, and on conviction shall be imprisoned in the penitentiary. . . ."
—TENNESSEE CODE 39-3301

"*A*lthough important decisions on abortion payments, racial quotas and the commercial use of genetic engineering attracted the most attention, the Supreme Court's 1979-80 term offered one overriding theme: **The expanding right of Americans to sue the government**.

"While seldom fodder for newspaper headlines, a citizen's power to hold government and its agents responsible for lawless actions is as essential to a republican form of government as is the power of the ballot."
—Richard Carelli,
Associated Press,
Washington, July 6, 1980

10
THE PROPER COURSE FOR GOVERNMENT

The position I recommend for state, county, and municipal officers under Constitutional Oath is this: accept paper money from all persons who tender it voluntarily, but do not attempt to enforce payment from those who raise the Constitutional objection.

This position lets you live with your conscience; it's reasonable, moral, and serves the cause of freedom. Some officials are relatively immune from economic fluctuations; cost of living raises keep them more or less comfortable in the most turbulent times. Besides, it may not be in your best interests to speak out. If you took *too* original a stand, you might suffer complicated reprisals from higher-ups. No, the key to financial liberation is properly in the hands of the *people*, the people you serve. Let them guide you.

If the people neglect to object to paper, take their money.

I regret saying it, but folks who labor under the illusion that they are powerless to correct their own misery *deserve* their misery. Persons who let their *right* be intimidated by *wrong* deserve intimidation. Persons who neglect to learn the benefits and privileges guaranteed by the Supreme Law of the Land *deserve* getting fleeced. Persons who don't know the difference between gold and paper don't know the difference between reality and dreams, so let them pay for living in the ideasphere by giving up their property to the tentacles of inflation. Let them get their satisfaction from complaining and contributing to toothless organizations.

On the other hand, persons who *know* the law and exercise their *rights* under the law are lawfully immune from enforcement of payment to any state or local agency of any amount of tender not declared to be the money of account of the United States.

Now, some officers might feel the temptation to answer objections to paper tender by denominating paper debts at current gold or silver quotations, so they can remain true to their oath of office. Here's the scenario: A taxpayer objects to a $600 property tax assessment in paper dollars, so the official levies the tax at one ounce of gold (say gold at that moment is $520 per ounce), plus small silver coins to make up the remainder. This is patently unfair: gold and silver prices on the free market fluctuate very capriciously from hour to hour. You'd be working an unlawful[1] hardship on the objector, while contributing to the erosion of the economy and your own fortunes as well, no matter *how* nice a cost-of-living-pay-raise deal you might have. The objector is *leading* you to high ground in the face of a flood. Don't fight him! Just go by the law.

The people—and *you*, too— are entitled to a constant and dependable value of gold and silver coin, **responsibly regulated by Congress, not the free market.**[2] That's the whole purpose of Article I Sections 8 and 10. The "free market," by the way, is not really a free market at all, but a

---

1. The tax is not assessed in gold and silver but in paper dollars.

2. This is not to say Congress should ignore the free market. Rather, its regulations should issue in response to free market prices of gold and silver as commodities, *buffering* us from the dangers of wild fluctuations. Is this not carrying out the Constitutional mandate to "promote the general welfare"?

handful of dignitaries who declare gold and silver prices each morning in a stately private boardroom in London. Whom are these gentlemen more interested in, you or themselves? If you disapproved of their mischief, how can you vote them out of office? With a Congressionally regulated gold and silver currency, you could specifically *un*vote those representatives who tampered with the value of your money.

What all this means is that knowledgeable persons, persons who object to paper money under Article I Sections 8 and 10 and who insist upon paying in the money of account of the United States are immune from all taxes, fees, debts of any kind under state authority until paper money is made redeemable in gold and silver coin. This is perfectly just. *Shouldn't obedience to law and truth contain a reward?* Isn't it fitting that economic benefits should flow abundantly upon those with the knowledge and courage to do the right thing by law?

History's paramount lesson is this: when tragedy gathers on the horizon, the knowers act to survive. Only the knowers survive. The knowers. The Noahs.

If you still doubt the authority of the people and Article I Section 10, consider these principles from *American Jurisprudence*, supported by cases too numerous to cite:

1. No public policy of a state can be allowed to override the positive guaranties of the Federal Constitution. (16 AmJur 2nd, 70)

2. No emergency justifies the violation of any of the provisions of the United States Constitution. (16 AmJur 2nd, 71)

3. Neither emergency **nor economic necessity** justifies a disregard of cardinal constitutional guaranties. (16 AmJur 2nd, 81)

4. Any attempt to do that which is prescribed in the Constitution in any manner other than that prescribed, or **to do that which is prohibited** is repugnant to that supreme and paramount law **and is invalid**. (16 AmJur 2nd, 82)

§155. As imposing obligatory duty.

Since the constitution is intended for the observance of the judiciary as well as the other departments of government and the judges are sworn to support its provisions, the courts are not at liberty to overlook or disregard its commands, or countenance evasions thereof. It is their duty in authorized proceedings to give effect to the existing constitution and to obey all constitutional provisions, irrespective of their opinion as to the wisdom or desirability of such provisions, and irrespective of the consequences.

If the constitution prescribes one rule and the statute another and a different rule, it is the duty of the courts to declare that the constitution, and not the statute, governs in cases before them for judgment.

—16 AMERICAN JURISPRUDENCE 2nd

". . . with a firm Reliance on the Protection of divine Providence, we mutually pledge to each other our Lives, our Fortunes, and our sacred Honor."

—A DECLARATION By the REPRESENTATIVES of the UNITED STATES OF AMERICA, In GENERAL CONGRESS Assembled, July 4, 1776

11
UNDER INVESTIGATION

One evening recently, at their request, I met with two Special Investigators from the Tennessee Department of Revenue at a favorite Sewanee hangout, *Shenanigan's*. They announced that their purpose for the meeting was to investigate me for possible criminal and civil violations of the Tennessee Revenue Code. Years ago, and repeatedly, I had asked the state to inform me what "Dollar" meant on the tax forms for my little theatre restaurant, but never got a comprehensible reply. So I looked up Federal statutes for a definition of "Dollar." No one had ever paid us in gold or silver, so I assumed we'd had no Dollar income and owed no Dollars.

One of the agents advised me of my right to remain silent and to have an attorney. Then, he asked me my full name. I chose to remain silent on that, and on all other questions that would make their investigation into my finances a piece of cake.

Uniquely in America, we are under no obligation to provide information that can be used against ourselves. Further, the **fact** that we choose not to give information cannot be used against us, either. Silence can NOT presume guilt. Yet, how many Americans know this? Aside from Article I Section 10, the Fifth Amendment is the main reason I intend to remain forever an American person. It is the most wonderful guarantee of freedom from a malignant government in the whole world.[1]

I got the distinct feeling that the agents respected my using my Constitutional right against inquisition. They had heard my views on money before, back when they were investigating Rusty Leonard who had asked me along as a witness, and so tonight they started posing questions about money. Not MY money (I wouldn't answer those questions), but about money in general. They had been thinking about it, and wanted to know more. All three of us relaxed. Then I told them about Washington's letters during and after the great Continental Inflation. They hadn't known about that. They hadn't known about Judge Roger Sherman's reasons for Article I Section 10, either. I told them about all my unanswered (or evasively answered) correspondence with state people begging them for a definition of "Dollar" on state forms. I told them that as soon as an officer of the state showed me where I was wrong, I would mend my ways immediately. I also told them that they, as much as you and I, had the power to save their personal finances from exploding in their faces.

"But if we went to a redeemable currency," one of them said, "what would happen to the balance of payments, interest rates, the IMF, international trade, things like

---

1. The best job of educating Americans of their Fifth Amendment (and other) privileges under the Constitution is being done, not by our most distinguished universities, but by THE ARIZONA CAUCUS CLUB. Charles Riely, its Director, has asserted his Fifth Amendment privilege on his 1040 IRS forms since 1970, giving the government no information, paying no money. In 1979, he was tried in Federal District Court in Phoenix for willful failure to file *and was found innocent by a 12-person jury*. Chuck deserved the cover of both *Time* and *Rolling Stone* for this stunning proof that our Constitution gives one man greater power than the entire U.S. Justice Department and IRS combined, but the event was naturally black-listed by most of the media. The transcript of his trial is, in my opinion, as much a dramatic masterpiece as *Inherit The Wind*; it will make your heart soar and you will cheer. Write ARIZONA CAUCUS CLUB, P.O. Box 60, MESA, ARIZONA, 85201, for their complete list of the finest, latest, and most comprehensive constitutional materials on the market today, including the *US vs Riely Transcript*.

that?"

"If we had gold and silver money again," the other said, "wouldn't the banks go broke? Wouldn't all government collapse?"

That's the debate trap, I told them. Experts can filibuster day after day, week after week, month after month, year after year. **"What if" is the most potent weapon the Friends of Paper Money have.** Debate and indecision merely fertilize inflation.

The best illustration I could think of was believing in God. If you sit down and try to figure out the consequences of living by God's program, you'll be so busy projecting, calculating, figuring, you'll never get around to committing to Him. The way to believe in God, as any minister or priest will tell you, is assume He is Truth and just begin operating by His system, no questions asked. Like an automatic pilot. If Truth is good, then good things will happen to you. If Truth is good, should bad things threaten you you'll know innately how to ward them off.

Clinging to Truth. That's all. The simplest thing in the world. *Clinging to Truth automatically summons good consequences.* The right things just fall into line. Debates and indecision evaporate. You're free just to be happy. That's what God's all about, God and law and Truth. I've never known a person to choose God and be dissatisfied with his choice, have you? On the other hand, I've known many people who postpone and debate, postpone and debate, trying with their masters degree intellects to reason and predict outcomes. For their trouble, they seem always plagued with some inexplicable disorder. Some malfunction that needs attention. Their problem is that they try to evaluate in each situation which would be the more profitable act: the truthful or the untruthful. They are the prisoners and practitioners of Situation Ethics, and they're so busy with their constant inner debate they haven't the time to relax and enjoy the great beauty of life. For all their bother, about half their decisions poison them anyway.

The United States Constitution is so harmonious with the simplest unchangeable laws of nature that I wholeheartedly agree with those who consider it to be Divinely inspired. No other constitution of any other country in the world guarantees its people a government sworn to protect and defend *individual freedom*, freedom to be right, freedom to be wrong, and most importantly the freedom not to be tricked out of their property by some clever scheme. A clever scheme like paper currency promising redemption for gold and silver one day, then suddenly reneging on the promise after your precious metal has been taken away from you. Whether it's one week or *twenty years* before you feel the effects of such a dirty trick, you have the freedom to blow the scheme's cover whenever you've had enough.

And it's guaranteed right there in Article I Section 10, in those 17 magic words of Judge Sherman. Everybody else in the world is being systematically robbed of their property because they don't have a law against paper money. We have one, but we don't know it. We know batting averages and the biographies of movie stars, but we don't know we have a law against economic tragedy, a law every public official from Main Street to Pennsylvania Avenue is sworn to support.

So, I told my friends from the Revenue Department, you don't need to be overly informed on interest rates, international payments, bond issues, gold prices, silver futures, or other consequences; and you certainly don't have to debate the pros and cons of obeying the United States Constitution. The choice is as simple as clinging to Truth or to Untruth. God and justice, or confusion and perjury.

Just OBEY that God-inspired United States Constitution, *forget about the rest of the world* (is the rest of the world worrying about you?), and good things will happen to everyone beginning immediately. And in ways so vast and unexpected that they would be impossible to calculate in advance even at MIT.

Of course, some of the closer friends of paper money

might have to revise priorities just a little bit, but shouldn't they? *Shouldn't they pay a few dues after all they've charged us?*

The conversation lasted almost two hours, then reached a warm and friendly conclusion. As we were getting up to leave, one of them said, "That part about not having to be overly informed, just believing in God and everything else falls into line, that makes a great deal of sense to me."

Next evening, several good old boys who had been watching the interview apprehensively from the bar asked me if I'd been scared. "How can I be scared," I said, "when all I've done is obey a law those guys are sworn to uphold?"

"*I* deny the power of the general government to making paper money, or anything else a legal tender."
—Thomas Jefferson

"*The* public welfare demands that constitutional cases **must be decided according to the terms of our Constitution itself**, and not according to judges' views of fairness, reasonableness, or justice. I have no fear of constitutional amendments properly adopted, but **I do fear the rewriting of the Constitution by judges under the guise of interpretation**."
—Justice Hugo Black, in Columbia University's *Charpentier Lectures*, 1968

"*The* people can discern right, and will make their way to a knowledge of right . . . The appeal from the unjust legislation of today must be made quietly, earnestly, perseveringly; in a popular government injustice is neither to be established by force, nor to be resisted by force: in a word, the Union, which was constituted by consent, must be preserved by love."
—George Bancroft,
*Commemorative Oration
Upon the Death of Andrew Jackson*,
Washington,
June 27, 1845

12
PUTTING THE CONSTITUTION INTO YOUR EVERYDAY CONVERSATION

Now that you understand the differences between paper and lawful money, and between law and hearsay, you're in a position to discuss things with persons in government. Educate them. Most of them have never had anyone bring up the constitutionality of paper money before. Don't harangue them or be rude (as I confess I have done in the past). Remember, they've done nothing wrong as long as people are willing to give them paper without objecting to its lawlessness. Here are some little things you can do:

TALK IT UP

A letter to various state and local officials in your town or county—and to your state representatives—asking them if they enforce payment of taxes, fines, and other debts in anything other than gold and silver coin will alert them to the issue. And while you're at it, send a copy to your governor. Send your state's Attorney General a letter asking him for an opinion (he's obliged to respond): "Is Article I Section 10 of the U.S. Constitution still binding on this state?" *Get them all reading and talking.*

The subject is so touchy to many officials that they will probably answer you evasively, cunningly. In person, they may even make remarks and innuendos suggesting that you're nuts, but don't let this bother you. You're *right*, and they know it, rather "fear" it. They're afraid that if you win, the whole *universe* will cave in on their heads. They have this fear because they've been educated (like you and I) by the Friends of Paper Money to think the problem is "very delicate," "complicated," and completely out of their hands. **The ideasphere says the problem is solvable only by the celebrities in Washington.** For many decades, our state and local officials have been conditioned to feel inferior: they're not as famous, not as well-paid, not as internationally glamorous as the Washington dignitaries. This creates a helpless attitude.

It's up to you to show your Main Street public servants that they have incredible power. Show them how the Constitution was written to give THEM ALONE the power to calm America's wild economic thrashing. THEM ALONE. Only THEY can kill financial confusion dead in its tracks by restoring the solid foundation of gold and silver coin. Tell them about Article I Section 10 and about the money of account of the United States.

Mention to the checkout girls and other clerks you encounter in a typical day that the tax they're collecting from you is in unlawful money and that you're not kidding. They're conspiring with the state to violate the Constitution, tell them good-naturedly. Tell them that the reason food prices are soaring is that *increasing paper increases prices*, and that only the state can stop paper by refusing to make it a tender. Tell them that they and the state are illegally making something other than gold and silver coin a tender in payment of debt. The Constitution forbids enforcement of taxes by any state or local official in paper, plastic, copper, checks or bank digits. And you don't have any gold or silver, because the Federal Reserve won't give you any. (See APPENDIX, page 142.)

Tell them to ask old-timers if food prices don't remain relatively stable when paper is redeemable for gold and silver coin. Show them Article I Section 10. You could offer someone $1,000 to show you where that has been amended. You could even offer $10,000 to anyone who can show you a law that permits the state to circumvent Article I Section 10. You're 100% safe on both offers, as of 1980. You could offer a *million* and no one would be able to collect.

Discuss it with your priest or minister. The Constitution is the closest thing to Scripture there is. If it's the codification of the word of God in legal terms, it's certainly worth recommending from the pulpit and in counselling and in Sunday School. Worth studying daily.

AVOID CONGRESSMEN AND SENATORS

Don't bother your Congressman about a redeemable currency. He's probably the greatest Friend of Paper Money in the country today. If you really want to hear some uneasy, extremely cunning word-mincing, talk to your Congressman about restoring a gold and silver monetary system. I don't recommend it unless he happens to be willing—as a state citizen—to impose Article I Section 10 upon high officers in state government. If not, he has the perfect excuse for copping out.

Because the Constitution empowers Congress "to borrow money on the credit of the United States." In borrowing from the Federal Reserve System, your Congressman and Senator are *merely carrying out their Constitutional mandate*. Your representatives in Washington are sweethearts of the Federal Reserve. The Friends of Paper Money contribute *gobs* to *all* the candidates and entertain *lavishly* the winners once in office. That's why you rarely if ever hear a peep of criticism on the American banking system out of Washington. If anyone is criticized it's *you*, for "wasting" our natural resources and oil, for buying too many things, for enjoying life, etc.

What Congress can do is try to balance the budget, which amounts to little more than scolding imaginary villains in the ideasphere. And while Congress can't object to paper tender, it can enact legislation permitting the reduction of standards of quality in foodstuffs, investments, manufactured goods, and personal freedom—legislation requiring you to lower your standard of living in the name of "conservation"—for the express purpose of *enabling the value of your money to be further diminished.* Since your Washington representatives enjoy a virtual immunity from inflation through cost-of-living raises they vote for themselves, they simply don't *feel* the chaos and pain in the same way you do.

No, as famous, as majestic, as well-groomed, as omnipotent, as black-limousine *dignified* as Congress might seem in our minds, it is *absolutely helpless to initiate the action that will turn away the gathering tragedy.*

Don't waste your time with Washington on this.

AVOID VOTING

We Americans treasure our most prized possession: our vote. There's something slightly unpatriotic about someone who doesn't use his vote to determine the course of his republic. The media are filled with urgings to vote.

But what good is your vote if everyone up for election is ignoring the law? Won't more voters just hasten the chaos and confusion? If you were ignoring the law and were elected by a landslide, would you sense any inducement to stop ignoring the law?

When officials *abide* by the United States Constitution, the vote is our way of selecting the best persons and the best government. But if our officials are breaking the Constitution, or allowing it to be broken without lifting a finger, *your* vote is literally *their* license to steal. You are giving them permission to take your property and control your life. If you give them that permission, many will take you up on it, because lots of folks enjoy controlling others and amassing property. If you vote for anyone that allows Article I Section 10 to be ignored, don't you deserve to be ravaged by inflation?

The vote is only a small part of your influence over your public servants, and it only works when the Constitution's money system is in operation. You might as well stay home on election day as long as the Constitution's money system is in mothballs, because you'll only be voting for violators or accomplices. (Don't remove your name from the Registration Lists, though. You'd be giving up your right to serve on a jury, which is a thousand times more important than voting. On a jury, you become a judicial officer, with as much power as a judge!)

LAWYERS[1.]

My personal experience is that many lawyers are ignorant of the Constitution *as law*. They see the Constitution as the point of departure for Supreme Court "interpretations." To hear many lawyers tell it, the Constitution only means what the Supreme Court SAYS it means. This is pathetically untrue. This is living in the *legal* ideasphere. It's Supreme Court Worship. Abraham Lincoln complained about Supreme Court Worship in his First Inaugural Address:

> If the policy of the government upon vital questions affecting the whole people is to be fixed by decisions of the Supreme Court, then the people will have ceased to be their own rulers.

The Supreme Court can't make laws. The Constitution rules the Supreme Court, not the other way around. The Supreme Court is simply a final court of appeal that decides specific cases brought to it. It often refuses to hear

---

1. You shouldn't shrink from being your own lawyer. It's thrilling and it's fun, and more and more serious people are getting into it. The venerable and trustworthy Dr Martin Larson states: "Anyone who will follow the clear and simple instructions fully set forth in (the book) HOW TO BE YOUR OWN LAWYER will not only save a great deal of money; he will also gain a valuable education and may even be more successful in an actual court case than he would be by engaging the services of an expensive attorney." **HOW TO BE YOUR OWN LAWYER IN COURT** is available from **Citizen's Law Library**, 6 W. Loudoun Street, Leesburg, VA 22075, $14.95.

cases. Too, it often refuses to *judge* cases. Imagine having waited years for a Supreme Court decision and then getting a statement like this made by Justice Brandeis in *Ashwander v Tennessee Valley Authority*, 297 US 288:

> A judge, conscious of the fallibility of human judgment, will shrink from exercising in any case where he can conscientiously and with due regard to duty and official oath *decline the responsibility*.

Lawyers who depend too heavily on case law instead of the Constitution ought to be reminded that judges are sworn to support the *Constitution*, not case law.

I now feel apologetic for having criticized lawyers. After all, my father was one. I've got friends in the profession. Let me call on a *lawyer*, then, to criticize lawyers. T. David Horton, a member of the Nevada, the Virginia, and the District of Columbia bars, and a member of the United States 9th Circuit Court of Appeals, said:

> The course that lawyers take called 'Constitutional Law' frankly doesn't consist of studying the Constitution. It involves memorizing the catechism—studying the sophistries—by which one provision after another of our Constitution is construed out of existence. This is one reason why in our present constitutional crisis we find lawyers among those who are derelict, failing to advance any remedy to correct the situation. [1]

Mr. Horton then revealed the astonishing reason why lawyers are lacking in fundamentals of the United States Constitution. In the words of one young lawyer: "There are no questions on the bar examination on the Constitution, so why should we bother with it?" [2]

I'm afraid the first step in the restoration of America to happiness and economic prosperity will not, *can* not occur

---

1. A. E. Roberts, *The Republic: Decline and Future Promise*, Ft. Collins, Colo: Betsy Ross Press, p. 69.
2. *Ibid.*

in the voting booths, the Supreme Court, among our lawyers, or at the federal level. For our Constitution reserves the greatest amount of power not to dignitaries but to housewives and shop owners, workers, the people. Just plain folks. The miracle will happen right in your town, right there on Main Street, and you and a couple of friends will pull it off. As Charles Riely said, "It will not be the lawyers, politicians or bureaucrats who save America. It will be the people who work with their hands. Housewives, truckers, carpenters, and farmers will turn this country around."

And because my wife and I both have been in the profession, I would like to add *schoolteachers*.

"*Teenagers are more frequent crime victims than adults are now or were during their youthful years.*

"*Two of every five high school students are victims of violent crimes including robbery, assault, and murder.*"
— U.S. CENSUS BUREAU,
reported by John F. Sims in
Moneysworth, October, 1978

"*He who walks with wise men becomes wise.*"
— PROVERBS 13:20

"*You see, the more we are conditioned by education and just living in a society which teaches us to think along certain lines, the easier we are to fool. The magician encourages us to follow one logical path — the one we are accustomed to follow in a normal situation — while he, unknown to us, takes an entirely different one to accomplish his illusion. Thus, the hardest people to fool are children, who take little for granted. The easiest are scientists.*"
— Charles Reynolds,
Magician's Consultant, *Parade*,
August 24, 1980

"*While young people are gathering flowers and nose gays, Let them beware of the snake in the grass.*"
— Roger Sherman,
Almanac, 1750, New York

13
A LESSON THEY'LL NEVER FORGET

Many of the ugly, ridiculous fixtures in public education parents and teachers feel so helpless to repair came about through the printing of paper money. Remember, it is paper money that makes possible dumb projects like busing. Constitutional money would stop the deterioration of our school systems in a snap.

In Tennessee and probably in your state, too, all public schoolteachers are required to take an oath to support the Constitution of the state and of the United States. In Tennessee, those teachers "who refuse to take the oath . . . shall be immediately dismissed from the service." (TCA 49-1304). I assume that the punishment for perjuring that oath would be as harsh as for refusing to take it, wouldn't you? Maybe even harsher. Both instances would certainly show a disregard for the Supreme Law of the Land, to the thinking of any reasonable person.

So if you're a Tennessee schoolteacher you're a duly sworn Constitutional officer! *You are prohibited from making any thing but gold and silver coin a tender in the payment of debts.* If you choose to take a paycheck of ever-depreciating paper when the law entitles you—requires you—to take gold and silver coin, what kind of model are you for young sensibilities?

Would you want *your* child to come under the daily influence of a person who couldn't tell the difference between a solid gold disc and a paper rectangle?

Even if you're not a sworn Constitutional officer of your state, you can have enormous effect. Rather than engage in abrasive strikes for *higher* pay, for example, you can simply hold out for *lawful* pay. (All people who receive paper money from cities, counties, or states could do this.) That way, you'll eliminate the need ever to have to strike again, because you'll be getting both higher *and* lawful pay. Pay that will hold its value year after year. Your pension will be worth something when you retire.

All that paperwork that's driving you nuts: it would stop expanding overnight with the restoration of gold and silver coin, soon slowing to a trickle with all other dumb projects. And you'll be free to settle down to what attracted you to school teaching in the first place: *helping youngsters learn*. Isn't that the true joy of teaching?

You could teach

THE LESSON OF
THE TUMBLE-BUGS,

the untold story of one of the world's earliest currency-manipulations:

These are scarabs,

little stones carved in the shape of beetles. The carvings were introduced into Egypt in 2200 B.C., after a great natural catastrophe destroyed much of the land. The Hyksos ("Shepherd Kings") brought the idea from Mesopotamia, the birthplace of central banking, writing, military conscription, world war, and juryless trials. It took less than five minutes for a carver to make a scarab; its equivalent in gold took many hours to mine and refine. The live beetle—we call them *Tumble-bugs* in Tennessee— rolls amorphous animal waste into perfect spheres, like reconstructing a destroyed planet into a brand new one. Tumble-bugs bury the spheres in the ground, enriching the soil. Because of their good work, and because their stone likenesses bore uplifting mottoes and names of officials (like all artificial "bank" money), the native Egyptians trusted in them. They freely, enthusiastically, traded their gold and silver for them.

Gradually, the Hyksos officials pulled the gold and silver off for themselves, leaving an ever-increasing supply of scarabs to circulate. Dream money. The scarabs became worth whatever the Hyksos said they were worth. Since officials determined the value of human labor, they could direct human beings to dumb projects, like the pyramids!

The pyramids (there are about 36 major ones in Egypt) may be beautiful and very scientific, but they really are quite dumb.[1] With a country's manpower building pyramids—or fighting a war or making costly things that get lost in outer space like today—agriculture operates at a

---

[1]. "Most Egyptologists conclude that the Pyramid was built as a tomb for some pharoah. No other reason is offered for piling up so massive a mound of masonry than to protect the dead Pharoah from grave robbers. Oddly, *this is the single function which neither the Great Pyramid, nor any of the others, managed to fulfill*, there being no reliable report of any body having been found in any of the pyramids." (Peter Tompkins, *Secrets of the Great Pyramid*, New York: Harper Colophon Books, p. 236)

bare minimum. This means scarce food. Scarce food means food must be controlled by a central bureau. The Hyksos used the Egyptians' own gold to buy grain from other nations; to eat, the Egyptians had to go, scarabs in hand, to the central storehouses and hope the officials were in a good mood.

So you see, controlling populations by lifting their money into the ideasphere is old, old, old. The same rules apply today. They apply for all time. There will always be attempts to hook people on artificial money.

Of all the lessons alert teachers could give on money, the most exciting one would be the LESSON OF LIVING BY THE CONSTITUTION. It would be an object lesson.

In Tennessee and in many other states it is a teacher's

duty, required by law, "To teach the Constitution of the United States and of the state . . . for the purpose of instructing all the children as to their privileges and duties under said constitutions and for the promotion of good citizenship." (TCA 49-1307) What a wonderful opportunity for your pupils to witness history in the making! You, their teacher, exercising your Constitutional Oath, demonstrating every American's economic rights, privileges, and duties in demanding that your paycheck be redeemable in gold and silver coin (Article I Section 10) at a value regulated by Congress (Article I Section 8)!

Your pupils would be seeing the power of the people flexing right there in the classroom and being felt and responded to under the Capitol Rotunda in Washington. Think of the confidence that would charge the atmosphere in your school!

Much of the material sent you from Washington is subtly designed to belittle you and your students, which is one of the reasons young people are so edgy and volatile. But the Supreme Law of the Land specifically provides that if *anyone* is to belittle *anyone*, it's to be the *other way around*. *You* belittle *Washington*! As you steadfastly abide by your Constitutional Oath your pupils will be experiencing firsthand how their teacher, a state officer armed with Roger Sherman's 17 words, can require Congress to take steps to restore a lawful economy to this country.

It will be one lesson they'll never forget.

"*Wisdom gives strength to the wise man more than ten rulers that are in a city.*"
—ECCLESIASTES 7:19

"*In America a new people had risen up without king, or princes, or nobles, knowing nothing of tithes and little of landlords, the plough being for the most part in the hands of free holders of the soil. They were more sincerely religious, better educated, of serener minds, and of purer morals than the men of any former republic. By calm meditation and friendly councils they had prepared a constitution which, in the union of freedom with strength and order, excelled every one known before; and which secured itself against violence and revolution by providing a peaceful method for every needed reform. In the happy morning of their existence as one of the powers of the world, they had chosen justice for their guide.*"

—George Bancroft, *History of the United States of America*, 1886

14
THE MIRACLE ON MAIN STREET

There must be a crisis for there to be a change. A slowly rolling gripe isn't enough. Hypothetical arguments aren't allowed in the courts. No, there must be a genuine crisis.

The Miracle will happen soon after a few people like you bring up the unlawfulness of the enforcement of paper as a tender in payment of debt right there on Main Street. A judge will not be able to enforce payment of a traffic ticket because Federal Reserve paper was objected to by the defendant. A chancellor will be unable to enforce a judgment in a lawsuit because Federal Reserve paper was objected to by the defendant. A property tax goes unpaid because the taxpayer objects to the unlawfulness of checkbook money as a tender in the payment of debts. Out on the Interstate, a trucker objects to the tender in which his tax is demanded at the chicken coop. Remember, "Since nothing but gold and silver coin is a legal tender, tender in bank notes . . . if objected to will not be good." (LOWRY v McGHEE)

You ask the state's permission to violate Article I Section 10 so you can buy your automobile license plates, and permission is denied you. (No one can grant you permission to violate the Constitution.) How can you pay for your license? Is the state not forcing you to drive illegally? Will the state *give* you your plates at no charge? Others object to sales taxes collected by clerks at retail counters in money prohibitable by the state.

As the customer arrives at the grocery checkout counter, she addresses the cashier with the innocent words, "This will be a tax-exempt sale, please." Because many retailers make dozens of tax-exempt sales every day, the state provides them a form on which each tax-exempt customer records his name, tax number, and purchase amount. The cashier automatically refrains from calculating the sales tax into tax-exempt totals, and routinely hands the customer the tax-exempt form list. The customer enters her name, telephone number (since she has no tax number), and the words

>OBJECTION TO SALES TAX
>UNDER ARTICLE I SECTION 10,
>U.S. CONSTITUTION. IF QUESTIONED,
>PLEASE CALL.

The transaction is quiet, lawful, orderly, and financially rewarding for, in these days of hundred-dollar grocery baskets, a 6-to-10% savings isn't exactly chickenfeed!

The same approach is used in paying bills by mail. Sales taxes are subtracted from the total amount owed, with the polite notation on the return stub

>OBJECTION TO SALES TAX
>UNDER ARTICLE I SECTION 10,
>U.S. CONSTITUTION. IF QUESTIONED,
>PLEASE CALL.

(Of course, you know what you're doing, so you *want* them to call; it's part of the education process. But, I regret to say, they most probably won't.)

The mounting number of tax-exempt sales creates a paperwork nuisance for cashiers and managers, and so. . . .

A mounting number of retailers discontinues collecting sales taxes from their customers. The law actually *protects* retailers who object to unlawful paper tender, at least in

Tennessee and probably in your state, too. Tennessee law states:

> The tax hereby imposed shall be collected by the retailers from the consumer insofar as it can be done. *TCA 67-3020 (d).*

The phrase *insofar as it can be done* means "if the state cannot enforce payment in paper or copper money, and if there is no way of redeeming paper and copper dollar for dollar for gold or silver coin, tax collection by retailers *cannot be done.*"

(If you can afford the luxury of a small law library, get hold of your state's Code and become familiar with it. A set of the Tennessee—or your state's—Code Annotated costs less than Encyclopedia Britannica and takes up about the same shelf space. Law secretaries can point you to good used sets.)

Meanwhile, a group of schoolteachers refuses to accept inflation-causing checkbook money from the state. The Commissioner of Education, who receives and administers all federal funds, is forced to honor his Constitutional Oath and stand tall against "any thing but gold and silver coin" as tender in payment of federal debts to his state. Other groups of state employees object to being paid in bank-digit paper; some of the better-organized factions strike for lawful pay. . . .

Instead of paying their bills to incorporated businesses, consumers begin sending notes asking how a corporation, being an extension of the state, can make any thing but gold and silver coin a tender in payment of debts. If corporations are creatures of the state, existing by virtue of state charter, are they not as bound to obey Article I Section 10 as the states are? Corporations would be completely helpless in enforcing payment in irredeemable paper; and of what advantage would it be for them to sue for collection if the courts cannot enforce their judgments in any thing but the money of account of the United States, which—since Congress failed to declare what replaced gold and silver as that money—is... *nothing?*

Just as the Friends of Paper Money withdrew gold and silver from circulation, the people on Main Street begin withdrawing from their obligations to pay debts in a form of money prohibited by law.

This is economic justice.

The resolution to the crisis will be almost laughably simple. If you think that restoring silver or gold to our monetary system will require a difficult and tortuous journey through the corridors of Congress, read the United States Attorney General's published opinion, attached to 31 USC 311 in the federal statutes:

Unlimited coinage of silver

> The President has authority to proclaim and put into effect a plan for the unlimited coinage...of domestic silver produced after the effective date of the proclamation.
> —1933, 37 Op. Atty. Gen. 344, at 31 USC 311.

And so, appropriate state authorities will inform the President that their state is having trouble with its commercial and public revenues because the people are standing on the Constitutional prohibition against irredeemable paper. (I'll give a prize to the first state to reach the White House with this complaint. Keep me posted of your advances, by all means; you can reach me through Spencer Judd, Publishers.)

With the utterance of a few words and the flourish of a pen, our money will be locked into a permanent value. *Inflation will literally be scribbled away with the signing of a man's name.* I suspect, in fact, that the Proclamation is already written and that new redeemable paper notes have already been prepared and are simply waiting for you to call them out.

You must understand, though, that it is not *your* responsibility to petition the President for redeemability. It is your state's. You've got better things to do with your time and energy. The state is your *servant*, remember. Let your *servant* do the work.

Redeemability will be restored in the way redeemability has always been restored. It's a very routine operation, and the Friends of Paper Money know it by heart. They've been doing it for centuries.

The new paper will be *United States Treasury* money, and it will be redeemable dollar for dollar in gold and silver coin. Irredeemable Federal Reserve paper may still be used, worth a fraction of its value today, but I imagine most of it will simply be traded in and burned. There will probably be new Federal Reserve paper, too, if the Fed people can escape the restoration with their reputations intact. It will promise redemption just like the United States Treasury money. It will be a very smooth transition with no hard feelings if it happens before the tragedy.

If the Miracle were to happen as I write this, one United States Note would be worth one dollar of silver or 13 Federal Reserve paper dollars. The new pricing would be denominated in both new United States Notes and old Federal Reserve paper. Since paper and silver and gold would be exchangeable again, there would be no need to hoard precious metals, and we'd once again be able to experience that delicious sound of silver coins ringing on countertops. Our beautiful real money would creep out of hiding.

A gallon of gas would cost $1.30 Federal Reserve paper or one silver dime. Imagine gasoline at 10¢ a gallon! A can of tuna fish, about a dime, too. A great suit of clothes $20 United States notes, or $260.00 Federal Reserve paper.

Stable prices, year after year.

The American Dream would be over before it lapsed into madness. The monetary system that allows dreamers to snap their fingers and have funds for whatever they can scheme up without any concern for whether there is demand or need for it would be gone. The monetary system that creates Viet Nams and subsidizes drug addiction and all its crime and family-shattering and heartbreak would be gone. The monetary system that delivers control of your property to officials who use that control to foment idlers against you, the monetary system that drives truckers and pricing boys and small businessmen and elderly pensioners and struggling young couples crazy, the monetary system that makes rich men out of debtors and poor men out of savers, that rewards incompetency and unexplained projects, that makes perversity the fashion, that celebrates the flames of violence, that favors untruth over truth, this system would be gone. The Friends of Paper Money would be free to invest solid money in worthwhile projects people really want.

And, miraculously, *no one* would be hurt. Value would return. There would not only be jobs galore, but jobs doing things for which there is real demand. Genuine pride of workmanship would be naturally restored. A person's value would again be determined by his good deeds, not by his inside connections or his knack for finagling and covering up.

Because a sense of the value of one's property would be restored, a sense of privacy, too, would return. With a healthy sense of privacy comes a natural revulsion for pornography, which is but a low regard for both privacy and property. An esteem for one's own property and privacy naturally turns one's attentions away from celebrities in whose lives we are invited to live vicariously. Who needs to live in a celebrity's life or in a soap opera's plot when his *own* life has value, esteem, interest, and excitement?

Gold and silver coin, being rare, precious, and easily accounted-for, automatically guarantees wise and prudent government spending. Violators are easily detected, dishonored and removed from office. (Because it is impossible to account for artificial money, corruption flourishes in a paper economy.)

With gold and silver money, the United States budget would be self-balancing.

The people would express needs to one another and fulfill them among themselves, without government assistance. Costly projects no one wants (no one, that is, except their lobbyists) would shrivel and blow away for lack of demand.

Hands once considered untalented would begin turning out marvelous products. The joyous return of . . . *quality*!

Our children would grow up knowing they have genuine value. Because we rejected money that said "I don't know what I'm worth," we would stop hearing our teenagers say "I don't know what I want to do." The "use me" aimlessness of adolescence would vanish and leave solid purpose. Cheating would become deplorable again, instead of quasi-honorable as it is in many circles. The love between boy and girl would cease to be a make-out project and would become instead a sensitive comparison of real values. Marriages would be built not on dreams but on facts and abilities. Conversation would make sense. Life would become too thrilling for dope.

There would no longer be a need to seek escape, since being here would be so real and delightful and rewarding.

Our lives would be so *worth living* that suicide would be reduced as an option among the cures of our ills. Suicide and paper money march side by side throughout history. Since the most important plank of the Communist Manifesto is control of a country's wealth through issuance of paper money from a central bank, our restoration of Constitutional money will eliminate communism and socialism as menaces to our freedom. They won't even make interesting topics in news, in classrooms, or debate.

Perhaps the greatest relief would be felt by those public servants who today suffer from the nagging awareness that they are living a lie; at last, they'd be free of the terrible pressures of covering up their sins against the Constitution, the Supreme Law of the Land they have pledged their honor to support.

Yes, everyone will benefit from the Miracle: bureaucrats, rich, poor—even the Friends of Paper Money. We know this because gold and silver money *invariably* benefits all resourceful people.

The Constitution is our positive proof!

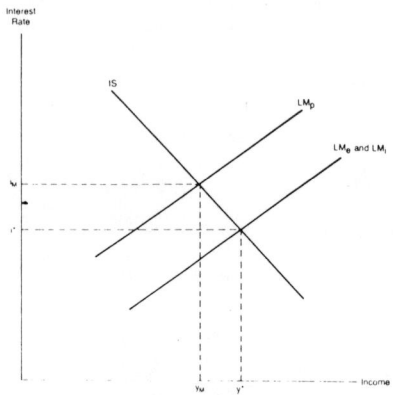

"ECONOMETRICS": WHAT YOU DON'T KNOW IS HURTING YOU

PAPER MONEY BENEFITS intellectual theorists at the expense of workers who produce goods. These charts, published February 1980 in *Issues In Monetary Policy* by the Research Division, Federal Reserve Bank of Kansas City, Thomas E. Davis, Senior Vice President, require vast special training and "inside" knowledge to be understood. Do you understand them?

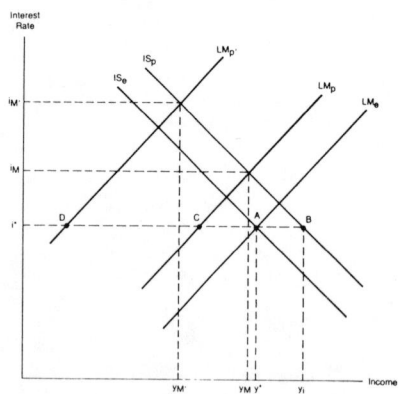

Paper money creates a "paper nobility" made up of information-brokers and speculators who extract great wealth from *changes* in value. But the United States Constitution did away with paper, nobility *and* changes in value.

With Article I Section 10 the Constitution established "the use of both gold and silver as standard money to insure the equal power of

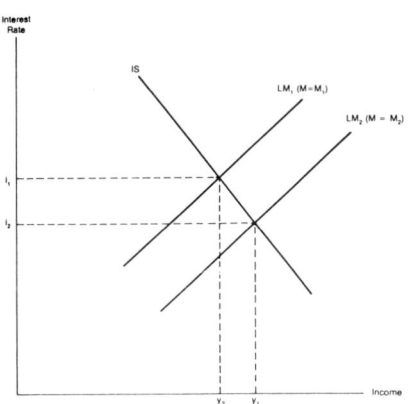

every dollar at all times in the markets and in the payment of debts." (This policy is found in federal law at 31 USC 311.)

Although the Constitution defined money once and for all time as "gold and silver coin," the Federal Reserve System "regularly publishes data for five alternative money definitions. Multiple measures

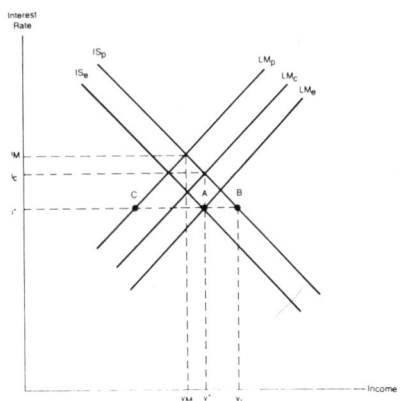

are published because there are differences of opinion as to what is the appropriate basis for defining money," according to *Issues In Monetary Policy.*

Whose definition will the courts be forced to uphold: the Federal Reserve's or the Constitution's?

"God did not make death, and he does not delight in the death of the living; the generative forces of the world are wholesome and there is no destructive poison in them."
—The WISDOM OF SOLOMON,
1: 13, 14

15
UNDERSTANDING GOVERNMENT FOR WHAT IT REALLY IS

Contrary to what TV, magazines, radio, and newspapers say, government is meant to occupy a very small part of our experience. (We must always remember that the media are usually beholden to government, or think they are.)

Man has existed for a million years, and he's only had government about 5,600 years. So government has occupied only a very small part of man's natural history. But in those 5,600 years government has done considerable damage. It has done lots toward pruning our species.

A Norwegian statistician computes that in these 56 centuries man has fought 14,531 wars. This is 2.6 wars per year. More than 600,000,000 men, women, and children have been killed by government. (I dread to compute how many people our own government has exterminated.)

In more than 880 generations, there have been no more than 10 meagre years of true peace. Think about that.

There is an old legal maxim "No man shall be without law." Government arises out of man's need for law. If man cannot govern himself, officials rush in to do it for him. There is always that constant pressure to have law, natural or otherwise. One of the great life-serving purposes of government, I believe, is to *test* man's need for law. If man *needs* law, if he fails to show that he can take care of himself and his own, government overcomes him. This is consistent with the way things work in nature. If a rabbit shows that he cares so little for life that he relaxes his vigilance, the eagle moves upon him.

Since governments live by virtue of helpless people, governments invest in keeping people helpless. The best way to keep people helpless is *to tell them constantly how helpless they are.*

Show them much crime, much menace, much mental derangement, much accidental death, much violence. Frighten them. Demonstrate to them how the only resolution to their dilemma is government. Send them to lawyers and accountants sympathetic or beholden to government. Circulate the proverb "You can't beat city hall." Oppress them, expropriate them, and then . . .

And then, what? Where does it lead? Once government has finally oppressed and expropriated every last soul on this planet, a strange phenomenon will happen. Oppression is not natural. Animals in cages live only a fraction as long as they live in the wild. Pretty soon, that world government will be faced with the ugly problem of death as a way of life. The leaders of government will have made a menagerie of dead animals. Everywhere they look, nothing but death and near-death. The architects of tyranny will grow miserable with their handiwork.

And that proposition reveals a solid gold secret. For, you see, government, that bloody beast of 600,000,000 corpses, *loves* strong people able to govern themselves. Although spokesmen will never tell you so, government *loves free people able to resist government.* This is why so many of our laws have little loopholes in them that excuse free people, people with so healthy and overpowering a determination to be naturally independent of government that they automatically spot legal clauses that strike discord with the higher, simpler law of God. Government admires, *cele-*

brates the fitness of people who are able to govern themselves, just like Hemingway admired, *loved* the Great Fish for escaping in the final moment of that brutal struggle in *Islands in the Stream*. But it is government's duty to challenge the individual, to test his mettle, to determine for certain the depth of his convictions and abilities.

This is natural selection.

Government chains, cages, or consumes the ones who surrender under its fearful threats and examples, but is most fond of the few that legitimately get away. These are the memorable ones.

Government propaganda likes to refer to any motion contrary to the prevailing drift as "rebellion" or "revolution" or "strike." Fearful words, words that make you tremble. Who wants to get involved in a rebellion? Leave that kind of monkey business to the rabble rousers.

This little book doesn't advocate any kind of insurrection whatsoever. As I told you earlier, you can make a lifesaving miracle happen simply by declining to break a law. If that's rebellion, then things really ARE topsy-turvy.

Here, in summary form, is what you have read:

1. **Irredeemable paper money** is the only cause of your family's growing financial distress.

2. **There is absolutely no cure** for irredeemable paper money except to make it redeemable in gold and silver coin.

3. **You have an undebatable**, specific, ironclad Constitutional right to enjoy a money of gold and silver coined and regulated in value by your representatives and senators in Congress.

4. **Absolutely no one** has the power to require Congress to provide us this solid money system immediately except your state and local government officials. Only *they*—not Congressmen—are prohibited from making paper a tender

in the payment of debts.

5. **Your state and local government** officials will not act until *you* tell them to. Most of them are completely unaware of their power over the United States Congress and the Federal Reserve Board. Remember, they suffer from propaganda fallout, too.

6. **The Declaration of Rights** of most state Constitutions guarantees you the indefeasible and unalienable right to see that your local and state officers obey their Constitutional Oath. Certainly the U.S. Constitution does. Would this right not include withholding payment of any state, local or corporate debts in a tender prohibited by the U.S. Constitution? Or demanding that state and local government and corporate paychecks be denominated in redeemable currency?

7. **The law requires all public** offices and courts to keep and have their accounts and proceedings in dollars of the money of account of the United States. Federal Reserve paper money has never been declared to be the money of account of the United States; it functions as such only because we *allow* the law to be ignored by our officials. No court or administrative official has any lawful authority whatsoever to require you to pay in something other than the money of account of the United States.

8. **Once redeemability is restored**, you and your family will immediately enjoy a "sense of prosperity and tranquillity that could hardly have been hoped for." You have George Washington's word on it.

9. **Redeemability will cause no sudden panics** or painful reversals of fortune for *anybody*, not even the Friends of Paper Money. As I write this, Federal Reserve paper dollars are already *unofficially* redeemable (at coin shops) at about $13 to $16 per silver dollar, gold a little higher. With official redeemability, paper dollars would merely remain at this price, and would circulate alongside United States Notes, which would be redeemable dollar for dollar in silver and gold. Gradually, the Federal Reserve paper dol-

lars would be phased out of existence.

10. **You need to ask yourself seriously**: If you *neglect* to take advantage of your lawful, God-insured economic rights are you not neglecting God, and would you not *deserve* economic catastrophe?

"*A* new public opinion must be created privately and unobtrusively. The existing one is maintained by the press, by propaganda, by organization, and by financial influences which are at its disposal. The unnatural way of spreading ideas must be opposed by the natural one, which goes from man to man and relies solely on the truth of the thoughts and the hearer's receptiveness for new truth."
—Albert Schweitzer

"*F*or America the gates of revolution are shut and barred and bolted down, never again to be thrown open; for it has found a legal and a peaceful way to introduce every amelioration. The Constitution is to the American people a possession for all ages."
—George Bancroft, History of the United States of America, 1886

EPILOGUE:

THE ILLUSION OF STATUS QUO

When you finish reading a book recommending action, you ponder alternatives and say to yourself, "I can either do what the book says or maintain the status quo." Now, I personally like the status quo. I believe that pure *status quo* "situation as is" is the regime that produces the longest, happiest lives. Long live status quo. EXCEPT.

Except that under paper money status quo is just an illusion. For under paper, radical social change is going on with each crank of the printing press, social change *over which you have no control*. Social change that costs you energy, having to work harder to make ends meet. Social change that makes you tense, wondering if you'll be next to lose your job. Social change that costs you happiness, complaining about how angry the latest moral dip or dumb project has made you. Social change that costs you health and tranquillity, as a loved one slips out of control into booze or drugs or psychosis or crime or the draft or early death.

Embracing the status quo in a society with a fluctuating, crisis-plagued paper economy is like dancing on quicksand.

Less than two years before the day of his funeral, President John Kennedy signed into law under the pressure of the "Cuban Missile Crisis" a series of emergency measures. These measures stand today as Executive Orders, waiting to be invoked by whichever President decides (or whose advisors decide) we are in perilous times. The surest cause of perilous times through the past 56 centuries has been inflation. If you choose to maintain the status quo in an ever-rising tide of Federal Reserve paper, you are helping to create the right moment for these Executive Orders to be called into being. Signed on February 16 and February 27, 1962, these documents give the President complete dictatorial control over your life. He will exercise this control through a bureaucracy of unelected dignitaries and officials in the Office of Emergency Planning. **If they hurt you, you cannot vote them out of power.** You have no recourse. You have no choice but to submit to their wisdom and judgment.

The bureau's control over your life becomes effective, according to the language of the Executive Orders, "in any time of increased international tension or *economic or financial crisis.*"

Try to imagine yourself and your family living under these Executive Orders:

1. EXECUTIVE ORDER 10995 takes over all communications media.

2. EXECUTIVE ORDER 10997 takes over all electric power, petroleum, gas, fuel, and minerals.

3. EXECUTIVE ORDER 10998 takes over all food resources and farms.

4. EXECUTIVE ORDER 10999 takes over all means of transportation, controls highways and seaports.

5. EXECUTIVE ORDER 11000 drafts all citizens into work forces under governmental supervision.

6. EXECUTIVE ORDER 11001 takes over all health, welfare, and educational functions.

7. EXECUTIVE ORDER 11002 empowers the Postmaster Gen-

eral to register all citizens nationwide.

8. EXECUTIVE ORDER 11003 takes over all airports and aircraft.

9. EXECUTIVE ORDER 11004 takes over housing and finance authorities, designates areas to be abandoned as "unsafe," establishes new locations for populations, relocates communities, builds new housing with public funds.

10. EXECUTIVE ORDER 11005 takes over all railroads, inland waterways, and public storage facilities.

11. EXECUTIVE ORDER 11051 designates responsibilities of the Office of Emergency Planning, gives authorization to put the above orders into effect in times of increased international tension or economic or financial crises.

Under Richard Nixon, these Orders were combined into the single *Executive Order 11490*, which was polished up with a few minor amendments signed by Jimmy Carter on July 20, 1979. And all it takes to push the button on this bonecrushing machinery is for the President to declare an "economic or financial crisis."

Is there a chance the Miracle on Main Street could be the crisis that pushes the button? Of course not. The Miracle is a *lawful act*, or in Judge Sherman's words at the Constitutional Convention in Philadelphia in 1787 "a *favourable* crisis." It is a self-correcting, *liberating* crisis. As you turn paper into gold and silver, the rising line on the crisis graph suddenly turns down to earth. You cause the prompt and orderly restoration of enterprise, credit, tranquillity, and "prosperity that could hardly have been hoped for." *The Miracle is the disappearance of the grounds for invoking the dictatorship of those Executive Orders.* The Miracle is a *good* crisis, like finding God. Feelings would be so happy, any President shouting "Crisis! Crisis! Executive Order!" would be laughed at as a clown.

The Executive Order crisis is a different kind, made by government, not by the people. It's the kind of crisis where the rising line bursts out of the graph. It bursts out of the graph because the people don't object to paper money in the way that counts. If you won't bring the rising line down to earth, it can only be assumed you are delegating your authority to dignitaries. It doesn't matter whether you delegate your authority out of ignorance, or complacency, or an act of will: your silence in a worsening situation is evidence of *surrender of your lawful power*. It's your way of saying "I'm helpless." **You have handed the problem over to the officials, and they would be foolish not to deal with the problem in such manner as rewards officials first.** Of course, the best part of their reward is getting to control your life. I have many friends who can already perceive this happening. Do you?

Why shouldn't a population blessed with the constitutional power to stop economic disaster but which does not use that power, why shouldn't such a self-neglecting population be tyrannized head to toe? Why shouldn't the rabbit dozing in the open suffer the eagle?

So you see, hanging on to the status quo in increasingly lawless times is actually the most violent kind of revolutionary behavior. Not objecting to paper money is the most wild-eyed, trouble-making, rabble-rousing kind of social terrorism.

If your posture is "I just don't want any trouble," your only choice is to help perform the Miracle. For trying to ignore the gathering tragedy, not wanting to discuss it, is an *active contribution* to lawlessness and your own destruction. You'd might as well be carrying a gun, shooting your friends, looting their homes.

Article I Section 2 of the Tennessee Constitution expresses it more adamantly than I have:

> *Non-resistance against arbitrary power and oppression is absurd, slavish, and destructive of the good and happiness of mankind.*

With these words, the **law itself condemns you** as absurd, as a slave, and as a destroyer of good and happiness if you fail to resist the oppression and arbitrary valuation of lawless money.

What social action could *be more fun* than the Miracle on

Main Street? What social action could be more harmlessly exciting than using *the law* to stimulate your state to force the President to call our precious coin out of hiding? (Don't worry. It's still there, plenty of it.) The Miracle on Main Street is a hundred times safer than burning draft cards, or marching for decency, or burning crosses, or demonstrating for Civil or Equal Rights, or demonstrating against busing, or chasing Iranian students out of town. It's safer because there's no demonstrating necessary. It's a personal thing. It's between you and the folks down at City Hall, you and the folks behind the counters of the shops that open out on Main Street, you and your child's teacher, you and your supervisor, you and your friends, you and me. It's done not with courageous, bold proclamations but with *polite inquiries*: "What has this state declared to be legal tender in the payment of debts?" "Are you upholding your oath to support Article I Section 10?"

The Miracle on Main Street will be the only truly powerful social movement where courage and daring are *not* fundamental requirements. It will be performed not by rabble but by nice, God-respecting people, from school children to old timers. Especially old timers, who contributed silver coin to Social Security only to receive paper dividends that buy less and less with each passing day. If they put silver in, shouldn't they get silver out?

One thing you'll not have to do as you achieve the Miracle is *fight*. I believe the concept that personal liberty is something that must be "fought for" is an old, old figment of the ideasphere concocted by artful official propagandists.

Do you remember the widely-circulated conservative slogan of the 1960's, "I'd rather be dead than Red"? The actual effect of this patriotic-sounding sentiment was the exact opposite of its apparent intent. "I'd rather be dead than Red" prompted the more reasonable listener to begin calculating how many of his freedoms he could surrender to Communist invaders and still remain relatively comfortable. The phrase might as well have been coined by Khrushchev himself.

Official propagandists have always depicted freedom as something that must be earned through bloody ordeal. Look at such emblems of liberty as war movies, the wounded fifer and drummers marching in Revolutionary America, Jesus Christ nailed to the cross. What is the purpose of these emblems? To encourage us to follow their example? For all the reverence and thanksgiving and piety they might inspire, they fail to encourage me to do anything but seek an alternative to fighting or suffering or dying at the hands of a liberty-robber. I'm not a martyr, and I don't believe you are, either.

No, I believe images of bloody ordeal are carefully designed to challenge the public imagination with the demand

**THIS IS THE PRICE OF LIBERTY.
ARE YOU WILLING TO PAY IT?**

And most people — the *best* people, those who really love their families and enjoy every instant of being alive and healthy — decide the price is just a bit too high. And so they give up some liberty, some integrity, a few of their private rights, in order to avoid a fight. **What they overlook is that in the United States of America, bloody ordeal is not the price of liberty.** The Constitution ruled out the Fight for Rights when it was ratified in 1789. Our Constitution *guarantees* no fighting. It *guarantees* "against violence and revolution by providing a peaceful method for every needed reform," as George Bancroft wrote.

If our officials should act adversely to the Constitution, upsetting our tranquillity, we simply remind them that they are wandering from the law they are sworn to follow. We *remind* in America, not fight. Reminding is easier, more humane than fighting. Reminding is educational, bringing adversaries together in *understanding* rather than in *ordeal*.

The outcome is clean, profitable for all concerned, and there are no hard feelings.

No, there is no fight involved in the Miracle on Main Street. It's a social action for scaredy cats.

Now that you've read this little book, you've learned about our money and the one essential law governing that money. You know probably more than many, many economics experts about the lawfulness of American money. More even than many lawyers and judges and government officials and professors.

You now have the power to make the Miracle happen. Work it!

I
APPENDIX
STATE CONSTITUTIONS THAT GUARANTEE
THE PEOPLE THE RIGHT TO ALTER AND
ABOLISH GOVERNMENT
IN SUCH (PEACEABLE) WAY AS THEY **THINK** PROPER:

Alabama	New Jersey
Colorado	North Carolina
Connecticut	North Dakota
Idaho	Ohio
Iowa	Oklahoma
Kentucky	Oregon
Maine	Pennsylvania
Maryland	South Dakota
Massachusetts	Tennessee
Mississippi	Texas
Missouri	Utah
Montana	Virginia
New Hampshire	Wyoming

(As published by Legislative Drafting Research Fund,
Columbia University, New York. 1978)

II
APPENDIX
THE SUPREME LAW OF THE LAND

THE CONSTITUTION OF THE UNITED STATES

PREAMBLE
[THE SIX REASONS FOR HAVING GOVERNMENT]

We, the people of the United States, *in order to form a more perfect Union, establish justice, insure domestic tranquility, provide for the common defense, promote the general welfare, and secure the blessings of liberty to ourselves and our posterity, do ordain and establish this Constitution for the United States of America.*

ARTICLE I
[WHO MAKES LAWS AND HOW]

SECTION 1 All legislative powers herein granted shall be vested in a Congress of the United States, which shall consist of a Senate and a House of Representatives.

SECT. 2.   1. The House of Representatives shall be composed of members chosen every second year by the people of the several States, and the electors in each State shall have the qualifications requisite for electors of the most numerous branch of the State Legislature.

2. No person shall be a Representative who shall not have attained to the age of twenty-five years, and been seven years a citizen of the United States, and who shall not, when elected, be an inhabitant of the State in which he shall be chosen.

3. Representatives and direct taxes shall be apportioned among the several States which may be included within this Union, according to their respective numbers, which shall be determined by adding to the whole number of free persons, including those bound to service for a term of years and excluding Indians not taxed, three-fifths of all other persons. The actual enumeration shall be made within three years after the first meeting of the Congress of the United States, and within every subsequent term of ten years, in such manner as they shall by law direct. The number of Representatives shall not exceed one for every thirty thousand, but each State shall have at least one Representative; and until such enumeration shall be made, the State of New Hampshire shall be entitled to choose three; Massachusetts, eight; Rhode Island and Providence Plantations, one; Connecticut, five; New York, six; New Jersey, four; Pennsylvania, eight; Delaware, one; Maryland, six; Virginia, ten; North Carolina, five; South Carolina, five; and Georgia, three.

4. When vacancies happen in the representation from any State the Executive Authority thereof shall issue writs of election to fill such vacancies.

5. The House of Representatives shall choose their Speaker and other officers, and shall have the sole power of impeachment.

SECT. 3.   1. The Senate of the United States shall be composed of two Senators from each State, chosen by the Legislature thereof for six years; and each Senator shall have one vote.

2. Immediately after they shall be assembled in consequence of the first election, they shall be divided as equally as may be into three classes. The seats of the Senators of the first class shall be vacated at the expiration of the second year; of the second class at the expiration of the fourth year; and of the third class at the expiration of the sixth year, so that one-third may be chosen every second

year, and if vacancies happen by resignation, or otherwise, during the recess of the Legislature of any State, the Executive thereof may make temporary appointments until the next meeting of the Legislature, which shall then fill such vacancies.

3. No person shall be a Senator who shall not have attained to the age of thirty years, and been nine years a citizen of the United States, and who shall not, when elected, be an inhabitant of that State for which he shall be chosen.

4. The Vice President of the United States shall be President of the Senate, but shall have no vote, unless they be equally divided.

5. The Senate shall choose their other officers, and also a President *pro tempore*, in the absence of the Vice President, or when he shall exercise the office of President of the United States.

6. The Senate shall have the sole power to try all impeachments. When sitting for that purpose, they shall be on oath or affirmation. When the President of the United States is tried, the Chief Justice shall preside; and no person shall be convicted without the concurrence of two-thirds of the members present.

7. Judgment in cases of impeachment shall not extend further than to removal from office, and disqualification to hold and enjoy any office of honor, trust, or profit under the United States; but the party convicted shall nevertheless be liable and subject to indictment, trial, judgment, and punishment, according to law.

SECT. 4. 1. The times, places and manner of holding elections for Senators and Representatives shall be prescribed in each State by the Legislature thereof, but the Congress may at any time by law make or alter such regulations, except as to the places of choosing Senators.

2. The Congress shall assemble at least once in every year, and such meeting shall be on the first Monday in December, unless they shall by law appoint a different day.

SECT. 5. 1. Each House shall be the judge of the elections, returns and qualifications of its own members, and a majority of each shall constitute a quorum to do business; but a smaller number may adjourn from day to day, and may be authorized to compel the attendance of absent members, in such manner and under such penalties as each House may provide.

2. Each House may determine the rules of its proceedings, punish its members for disorderly behavior, and, with the concurrence of two-thirds, expel a member.

3. Each House shall keep a journal of its proceedings, and from time to time publish the same, excepting such parts as may in their judgment require secrecy; and the yeas and nays of the members of either House on any question shall, at the desire of one-fifth of those present, be entered on the journal.

4. Neither House, during the session of Congress, shall, without the consent of the other, adjourn for more than three days, nor to any other place than that in which the two Houses shall be sitting.

SECT. 6. 1. The Senators and Representatives shall receive a compensation for their services, to be ascertained by law, and paid out of the Treasury of the United States. They shall in all cases, except treason, felony, and breach of the peace, be privileged from arrest during their attendance at the session of their respective Houses, and in going to and returning from the same; and for any speech or debate in either House they shall not be questioned in any other place.

2. No Senator or Representative shall, during the time for which he was elected, be appointed to any civil office under the authority of the United States which shall have been created, or the emoluments whereof shall have been increased during such time; and no person holding any office under the United States shall be a member of either House during his continuance in office.

SECT. 7. 1. All bills for raising revenue shall originate in the House of Representatives; but the Senate may propose or concur with amendments, as on other bills.

2. Every bill which shall have passed the House of Representatives and the Senate shall, before it becomes a law, be presented to the President of the United States; if he approves, he shall sign it, but if not, he shall return it, with his objections, to that House in which it shall have originated, who shall enter the objections at large on their journal, and proceed to reconsider it. If after such reconsideration two-thirds of that House shall agree to pass the bill, it shall be sent together with the objections to the other House, by which it shall likewise be reconsidered, and if approved by two-thirds of that House, it shall become a law. But in all such cases the votes of both Houses shall be determined by yeas and nays, and the names of the persons voting for and against the bill shall be entered on the journal of each House respectively. If any bill shall not be returned by the President within ten days (Sundays excepted) after it shall have been presented to him, the same shall be a law, in like manner as if he had signed it, unless the Congress by their adjournment prevent its return, in which case it shall not be a law.

3. Every order, resolution, or vote to which the concurrence of the Senate and the House of Representatives may be necessary (except on a question of adjournment) shall be presented to the President of the United States; and before the same shall take effect, shall be approved by him, or being disapproved by him, shall be repassed by two-thirds of the Senate and House of Representatives, according to the rules and limitations prescribed in the case of a bill.

[WHAT CONGRESS CAN DO]

SECT. 8. The Congress shall have power:
1. To lay and collect taxes, duties, imposts and excises, to pay the debts and provide for the common defense and general welfare of the United States; but all duties, imposts and excises shall be uniform throughout the United States;
2. To borrow money on the credit of the United States;
3. To regulate commerce with foreign nations, and among the several States, and with the Indian tribes;
4. To establish a uniform rule of naturalization, and uniform laws on the subject of bankruptcies throughout the United States;
5. To coin money, regulate the value thereof, and of foreign coin, and fix the standards of weights and measures;
6. To provide for the punishment of counterfeiting the securities and current coin of the United States;
7. To establish post offices and post roads;
8. To promote the progress of science and useful arts, by securing, for limited times, to authors and inventors, the exclusive right to their respective writings and discoveries;
9. To constitute tribunals inferior to the Supreme Court;
10. To define and punish piracies and felonies committed on the high seas, and offenses against the law of nations;
11. To declare war, grant letters of marque and reprisal, and make rules concerning captures on land and water;
12. To raise and support armies, but no appropriation of money to that use shall be for a longer term than two years;
13. To provide and maintain a navy;
14. To make rules for the government and regulation of the land and naval forces;
15. To provide for calling forth the militia to execute the laws of the Union, suppress insurrections, and repel invasions;
16. To provide for organizing, arming, and disciplining the militia, and for governing such part of them as may be employed in the service of the United States, reserving to the States respectively the appointment of the officers and the authority of training the militia according to the discipline prescribed by Congress;
17. To exercise exclusive legislation in all cases whatsoever over such district (not exceeding ten miles square) as may by cession of particular States and the acceptance of Congress, become the seat of Government of the United States, and to exercise like authority over all places purchased by the consent of the Legislature of the State in which the same shall be, for the erection of forts, magazines, arsenals, dock-yards, and other needful buildings;—and
18. To make all laws which shall be necessary and proper for carrying into execution the foregoing powers, and all other powers vested by this Constitution in the Government of the United States,

or any department or officer thereof.

[WHAT THE UNITED STATES CAN'T DO]

SECT. 9. 1. The migration or importation of such persons as any of the States now existing shall think proper to admit, shall not be prohibited by the Congress prior to the year one thousand eight hundred and eight, but a tax or duty may be imposed on such importation, not exceeding ten dollars for each person.

2. The privilege of the writ of *habeas corpus* shall not be suspended, unless when in cases of rebellion or invasion the public safety may require it.

3. No bill of attainder or *ex post facto* law shall be passed.

4. No capitation or other direct tax shall be laid, unless in proportion to the census or enumeration herein before directed to be taken.

5. No tax or duty shall be laid on articles exported from any State.

6. No preference shall be given by any regulation of commerce or revenue to the ports of one State over those of another; nor shall vessels bound to, or from, one State be obliged to enter, clear, or pay duties in another.

7. No money shall be drawn from the Treasury but in consequence of appropriations made by law; and a regular statement and account of the receipts and expenditures of all public money shall be published from time to time.

8. No title of nobility shall be granted by the United States; and no person holding any office of profit or trust under them, shall, without the consent of the Congress, accept of any present, emolument, office, or title, of any kind whatever, from any king, prince, or foreign state.

[WHAT NO STATE CAN DO]

SECT. 10. 1. **No State shall** enter into any treaty, alliance, or confederation; grant letters of marque and reprisal; coin money; emit bills of credit; **make any thing but gold and silver coin a tender in payment of debts;** pass any bill of attainder, *ex post facto* law, or law impairing the obligation of contracts, or grant any title of nobility.

2. No State shall, without the consent of the Congress, lay any imposts or duties on imports or exports except what may be absolutely necessary for executing its inspection laws; and the net produce of all duties and imposts, laid by any State on imports or exports, shall be for the use of the Treasury of the United States; and all such laws shall be subject to the revision and control of the Congress.

3. No State shall, without the consent of Congress, lay any duty of tonnage, keep troops, or ships of war in time of peace, enter into any agreement or compact with another State, or with a foreign

power, or engage in war, unless actually invaded, or in such imminent danger as will not admit delay.

ARTICLE II
[CARRYING OUT THE LAWS]

SECTION 1. 1. The executive power shall be vested in a President of the United States of America. He shall hold his office during the term of four years, and, together with the Vice President, chosen for the same term, be elected as follows:

2. Each State shall appoint, in such manner as the legislature thereof may direct, a number of electors, equal to the whole number of Senators and Representatives to which the State may be entitled in the Congress; but no Senator or Representative or person holding an office of trust or profit under the United States shall be appointed an elector.

3. The electors shall meet in their respective States, and vote by ballot for two persons, of whom one at least shall not be an inhabitant of the same state with themselves. And they shall make a list of all the persons voted for, and of the number of votes for each; which list they shall sign and certify, and transmit, sealed, to the seat of the Government of the United States, directed to the President of the Senate. The President of the Senate shall, in the presence of the Senate and House of Representatives open all the certificates, and the votes shall then be counted. The person having the greatest number of votes shall be the President, if such number be a majority of the whole number of electors appointed; and if there be more than one who have such majority, and have an equal number of votes, then the House of Representatives shall immediately choose by ballot one of them for President; and if no person have a majority, then from the five highest on the list the said House shall in like manner choose the President. But in choosing the President, the votes shall be taken by States, the representation from each State having one vote; a quorum, for this purpose, shall consist of a member or members from two-thirds of the States, and a majority of all the States shall be necessary to a choice. In every case, after the choice of the President, the person having the greatest number of votes of the electors shall be the Vice President. But if there shall remain two or more who have equal votes, the Senate shall choose from them by ballot the Vice President.

4. The Congress may determine the time of choosing the electors and the day on which they shall give their vote, which day shall be the same throughout the United States.

5. No person except a natural born citizen, or a citizen of the United States, at the time of the adoption of this Constitution, shall be eligible to the office of President; neither shall any person be eligible to that office who shall not have attained to the age of

thirty-five years, and been fourteen years a resident within the United States.

6. In case of the removal of the President from office, or of his death, resignation or inability to discharge the powers and duties of the said office, the same shall devolve on the Vice President, and the Congress may by law provide for the case of removal, death, resignation, or inability, both of the President and Vice President, declaring what officer shall then act as President, and such officer shall act accordingly until the disability be removed, or a President shall be elected.

7. The President shall, at stated times, receive for his services a compensation which shall neither be increased nor diminished during the period for which he shall have been elected, and he shall not receive within that period any other emolument from the United States, or any of them.

8. Before he enters on the execution of his office, he shall take the following oath or affirmation:

"I do solemnly swear (or affirm) that I will faithfully execute the office of President of the United States, and will, to the best of my ability, preserve, protect, and defend the Constitution of the United States."

SECT. 2.   1. The President shall be Commander-in-Chief of the Army and Navy of the United States, and of the militia of the several States, when called into the actual service of the United States; he may require the opinion, in writing, of the principal officer in each of the executive departments, upon any subject relating to the duties of their respective offices; and he shall have power to grant reprieves, and pardons for offenses against the United States, except in cases of impeachment.

2. He shall have power, by and with the advice and consent of the Senate, to make treaties, provided two-thirds of the Senators present concur; and he shall nominate and, by and with the advice and consent of the Senate, shall appoint ambassadors, other public ministers and consuls, judges of the Supreme Court, and all other officers of the United States, whose appointments are not herein otherwise provided for, and which shall be established by law; but the Congress may by law vest the appointment of such inferior officers as they think proper in the President alone, in the courts of law, or in the heads of departments.

3. The President shall have power to fill up all vacancies that may happen during the recess of the Senate, by granting commissions which shall expire at the end of their next session.

SECT. 3. He shall from time to time give to the Congress information of the State of the Union, and recommend to their consideration such measures as he shall judge necessary and expedient; he may, on extraordinary occasions, convene both Houses, or either of them, and in case of disagreement between them with respect to the time of adjournment, he may adjourn them to such time as he shall think proper; he shall receive ambassadors and other public ministers; he shall take care that the laws be faithfully executed, and shall commission all the officers of the United States.

SECT. 4. The President, Vice President, and all civil officers of the United States, shall be removed from office on impeachment for, and conviction of, treason, bribery, or other high crimes and misdemeanors.

ARTICLE III
[JUDGING BY THE LAWS]

SECTION 1. The judicial power of the United States shall be vested in one Supreme Court, and in such inferior courts as the Congress may from time to time ordain and establish. The judges, both of the Supreme and inferior courts, shall hold their offices during good behavior, and shall, at stated times, receive for their services a compensation which shall not be diminished during their continuance in office.

SECT. 2. 1. The judicial power shall extend to all cases, in law and equity, arising under this Constitution, the laws of the United States, and treaties made, or which shall be made, under their authority;—to all cases affecting ambassadors, other public ministers and consuls;—to all cases of admiralty and maritime jurisdiction;—to controversies to which the United States shall be a party;—to controversies between two or more States;—between a State and citizens of another State;—between citizens of different States;—between citizens of the same State, claiming lands under grants of different States, and between a State, or the citizens thereof, and foreign States, citizens, or subjects.

2. In all cases affecting ambassadors, other public ministers and consuls, and those in which a State shall be a party, the Supreme Court shall have original jurisdiction. In all the other cases before mentioned the Supreme Court shall have appellate jurisdiction, both as to law and fact, with such exceptions and under such regulations as the Congress shall make.

3. The trial of all crimes, except in cases of impeachment, shall be by jury, and such trial shall be held in the State where the said crimes shall have been committed; but when not committed within any State the trial shall be at such place or places as the Congress may by law have directed.

SECT. 3. 1. Treason against the United States shall consist only in levying war against them, or in adhering to their enemies, giving them aid and comfort. No person shall be convicted of treason unless on the testimony of two witnesses to the same overt act, or on confession in open court.

2. The Congress shall have power to declare the punishment of treason; but no attainder of treason shall work corruption of blood, or forfeiture except during the life of the person attainted.

ARTICLE IV
[INTERSTATE RELATIONS]

SECTION 1. Full faith and credit shall be given in each State to the public acts, records, and judicial proceedings of every other State. And the Congress may by general laws prescribe the manner in which such acts, records and proceedings shall be proved, and the effect thereof.

SECT. 2. 1. The citizens of each State shall be entitled to all privileges and immunities of citizens in the several States.

2. A person charged in any State with treason, felony, or other crime, who shall flee from justice and be found in another State, shall, on demand of the Executive authority of the State from which he fled, be delivered up, to be removed to the State having jurisdiction of the crime.

3. No person held to service or labor in one State, under the laws thereof, escaping into another, shall, in consequence of any law or regulation therein, be discharged from such service or labor, but shall be delivered up on claim of the party to whom such service or labor may be due.

SECT. 3. 1. New States may be admitted by the Congress into this Union; but no new State shall be formed or erected within the jurisdiction of any other State; nor any State be formed by the junction of two or more States, or parts of States, without the consent of the Legislatures of the States concerned, as well as of the Congress.

2. The Congress shall have power to dispose of and make all needful rules and regulations respecting the territory or other property belonging to the United States; and nothing in this Constitution shall be so construed as to prejudice any claims of the United States or of any particular State.

SECT. 4. The United States shall guarantee to every State in this Union a republican form of government, and shall protect each of them against invasion, and, on application of the Legislature, or of the Executive (when the Legislature cannot be convened), against domestic violence.

ARTICLE V
[HOW AMENDMENTS ARE TO BE MADE]

The Congress, whenever two-thirds of both Houses shall deem it necessary, shall propose amendments to this Constitution, or, on the application of the Legislatures of two-thirds of the several States, shall call a convention for proposing amendments, which, in either case, shall be valid to all intents and purposes, as part of this Constitution, when ratified by the Legislatures of three-fourths of the several States, or by conventions in three-fourths thereof, as the one or the other mode of ratification may be proposed by the Congress; provided that no amendment which may be made prior to the year one thousand eight hundred and eight shall in any manner affect the first and fourth clauses in the Ninth Section of the First Article; and that no State, without its consent, shall be deprived of its equal suffrage in the Senate.

ARTICLE VI

1. All debts contracted and engagements entered into before the adoption of this Constitution, shall be as valid against the United States under this Constitution, as under the Confederation.

[THE SUPREMACY CLAUSE]

2. This Constitution and the laws of the United States which shall be made in pursuance thereof; and all treaties made, or which shall be made, under the authority of the United States, shall be the supreme law of the land; and the judges in every State shall be bound thereby, anything in the Constitution or laws of any State to the contrary notwithstanding.

[THE BINDING OATH]

3. The Senators and Representatives before mentioned, and the members of the several State Legislatures, and all executive and judicial officers, both of the United States and of the several States, shall be bound by oath or affirmation to support this Constitution; but no religious test shall ever be required as a qualification to any office or public trust under the United States.

ARTICLE VII
[THE PEOPLE'S "YES"]

The ratification of the Convention of nine States shall be sufficient for the establishment of this Constitution between the States so ratifying the same.

Done in Convention by the Unanimous Consent of the States present the Seventeenth Day of September in the Year of Our Lord one thousand seven hundred and eighty-seven, and of the Independence of the United States of America the Twelfth. In witness whereof we have hereunto subscribed our names. [Ages added.]

GEO[RGE] WASHINGTON, 55
 President and deputy from
 Virginia

NEW HAMPSHIRE
 John Langdon, 46
 Nicholas Gilman, 32

MASSACHUSETTS
 Nathaniel Gorham, 49
 Rufus King, 32

CONNECTICUT
 William Samuel
  Johnson, 59
 Roger Sherman, 66

DELAWARE
 George Read, 53
 John Dickinson, 55
 Jacob Broom, 35
 Gunning Bedford, Jr., 40
 Richard Bassett, 42

MARYLAND
 James McHenry, 34
 Daniel Carroll, 31
 Daniel of St. Thos. Jenifer, 64

VIRGINIA
 John Blair, 55
 James Madison, Jr., 36

NEW YORK
 Alexander Hamilton, 30

NEW JERSEY
 William Livingston, 63
 David Brearley, 42
 William Patterson, 42
 Jonathan Dayton, 26

PENNSYLVANIA
 Benjamin Franklin, 81
 Robert Morris, 53
 Thomas Fitzsimmons, 46
 James Wilson, 45
 Thomas Mifflin, 43
 Gouverneur Morris, 35
 Jared Ingersoll, 37
 George Clymer, 48

NORTH CAROLINA
 William Blount, 38
 Hugh Williamson, 51
 Richard Dobbs Spaight, 29

SOUTH CAROLINA
 James Rutledge, 48
 Charles Pinckney, 29
 Charles Cotesworth
  Pinckney, 41
 Pierce Butler, 43

GEORGIA
 William Few, 39
 Abraham Baldwin, 32

ATTEST:
William Jackson, Secretary

The Constitution was declared in effect on the first Wednesday in March, 1789. Why isn't the first Wednesday in March an American holiday? Shouldn't it be?

AMENDMENTS TO THE CONSTITUTION OF THE UNITED STATES
PREAMBLE

The Conventions of a number of the States, having at the time of their adopting the Constitution, expressed a desire, in order to prevent misconstruction or abuse of its powers, that further declaratory and restrictive clauses should be added: that as extending the ground of public confidence in the Government, will best insure the beneficent ends of its institution.

AMENDMENT I

Congress shall make no law respecting an establishment of religion, or prohibiting the free exercise thereof; or abridging the freedom of speech or of the press; or the right of the people peaceably to assemble, and to petition the Government for a redress of grievances.

AMENDMENT II

A well-regulated Militia, being necessary to the security of a free State, the right of the people to keep and bear arms, shall not be infringed.

AMENDMENT III

No Soldier shall, in time of peace be quartered in any house, without the consent of the owner, nor in time of war, but in a manner to be prescribed by law.

AMENDMENT IV

The right of the people to be secure in their persons, houses, papers, and effects, against unreasonable searches and seizures, shall not be violated, and no warrants shall issue, but upon probable cause, supported by oath or affirmation, and particularly describing the place to be searched, and the persons or things to be seized.

AMENDMENT V

No person shall be held to answer for a capital, or otherwise infamous crime, unless on a presentment or indictment of a grand jury, except in cases arising in the land or naval forces, or in the militia, when in actual service in time of war or public danger; nor shall any person be subject for the same offense to be twice put in jeopardy of life or limb, nor shall be compelled in any criminal case to be a witness against himself; nor be deprived of life, liberty, or property, without due process of law; nor shall private property be taken for public use, without just compensation.

AMENDMENT VI

In all criminal prosecutions, the accused shall enjoy the right to a speedy and public trial, by an impartial jury of the State and district wherein the crime shall have been committed, which district shall have been previously ascertained by law, and to be informed of the nature and cause of the accusation; to be confronted with the witnesses against him; to have compulsory process for obtaining witnesses in his favor, and to have the assistance of counsel for his defense.

AMENDMENT VII

In suits at common law, where the value in controversy shall exceed twenty dollars, the right of trial by jury shall be preserved, and no fact tried by a jury, shall be otherwise reexamined in any court of the United States, than according to the rules of the common law.

AMENDMENT VIII

Excessive bail shall not be required, nor excessive fines imposed, nor cruel and unusual punishments inflicted.

AMENDMENT IX

The enumeration in the Constitution, of certain rights, shall not be construed to deny or disparage others retained by the people.

AMENDMENT X

The powers not delegated to the United States by the Constitution, nor prohibited by it to the States, are reserved to the States respectively, or to the people.

SUBSEQUENT AMENDMENTS

AMENDMENT XI

The judicial power of the United States shall not be construed to extend to any suit in law or equity, commenced or prosecuted against one of the United States by citizens of another State, or by citizens or subjects of any foreign State.

(Proposed to the Legislatures of the several States by the Third Congress on the 5th of March, 1794, and declared to have been ratified by Executive Proclamation, January 8, 1798.)

AMENDMENT XII

The electors shall meet in their respective States, and vote by ballot for President and Vice President, one of whom, at least, shall not be an inhabitant of the same State with themselves; they shall name in their ballots the person voted for as President, and in distinct ballots the person voted for as Vice President; and they shall make distinct lists of all persons voted for as President, and of all persons voted for as Vice President, and of the number of votes for each, which lists they shall sign and certify, and transmit sealed to the seat of the Government of the United States directed to the President of the Senate; the President of the Senate shall, in the presence of the Senate and House of Representatives, open all the certificates and the votes shall then be counted; the person having the greatest number of votes for President, shall be the President, if such number be a majority of the whole number of electors appointed; and if no person have such majority, then from the persons having the highest numbers not exceeding three on the list of those voted for as President, the House of Representatives shall choose immediately, by ballot, the President. But in choosing the President, the votes shall be taken by States, the representation from each State having one vote; a quorum for this purpose shall consist of a member or members from two-thirds of the States, and a majority of all the States shall be necessary to a choice. And if the House of Representatives shall not choose a President whenever the right of choice shall devolve upon them, before the fourth day of March next following, then the Vice President shall act as President, as in the case of the death or other constitutional disability of the President. The person having the greatest number of votes as Vice President shall be the Vice President, if such number be a majority of the whole number of electors appointed, and if no person have a majority, then from the two highest numbers on the list, the Senate shall choose the Vice President; a quorum for the purpose shall consist of two-thirds of the whole number of Senators, and a majority of the whole number shall be necessary to a choice. But no person constitutionally ineligible to the office of President shall be eligible to that of Vice President of the United States.

(Proposed by the Eighth Congress on the 12th of December, 1803, declared ratified by the Secretary of State, September 25, 1804. It was ratified by all the States except Connecticut, Delaware, Massachusetts, and New Hampshire.)

AMENDMENT XIII

1. Neither slavery nor involuntary servitude, except as a punishment for crime whereof the party shall have been duly convicted, shall exist within the United States, or any place subject to their jurisdiction.
2. Congress shall have power to enforce this article by appropriate legislation.

(Proposed by the Thirty-eighth Congress on the 1st of February, 1865, declared ratified by the Secretary of State, December 18, 1865. It was rejected by Delaware and Kentucky; was conditionally ratified by Alabama and Mississippi; and Texas took no action.)

AMENDMENT XIV

1. All persons born or naturalized in the United States, and subject to the jurisdiction thereof, are citizens of the United States and of the State wherein they reside. No State shall make or enforce any law which shall abridge the privileges or immunities of citizens of the United States; nor shall any State deprive any person of life,

liberty, or property, without due process of law; nor deny to any person within its jurisdiction the equal protection of the laws.

2. Representatives shall be apportioned among the several States according to their respective numbers, counting the whole number of persons in each State, excluding Indians not taxed. But when the right to vote at any election for the choice of electors for President and Vice President of the United States, Representatives in Congress, the executive and Judicial officers of a State, or the members of the Legislature thereof, is denied to any of the male inhabitants of such State, being twenty-one years of age, and citizens of the United States, or in any way abridged, except for participation in rebellion, or other crime, the basis of representation therein shall be reduced in the proportion which the number of such male citizens shall bear to the whole number of male citizens twenty-one years of age in such State.

3. No person shall be a Senator or Representative in Congress, or elector of President and Vice President, or hold any office, civil or military, under the United States, or under any State, who, having previously taken an oath, as a member of Congress, or as an officer of the United States, or as a member of any State Legislature, or as an executive or judicial officer of any State, to support the Constitution of the United States, shall have engaged in insurrection or rebellion against the same, or given aid or comfort to the enemies thereof. But Congress may by a vote of two-thirds of each House, remove such disability.

4. The validity of the public debt of the United States, authorized by law, including debts incurred for payment of pensions and bounties for services in suppressing insurrection or rebellion, shall not be questioned. But neither the United States nor any State shall assume or pay any debt or obligation incurred in aid of insurrection or rebellion against the United States, or any claim for the loss or emancipation of any slave; but all such debts, obligations, and claims shall be held illegal and void.

5. The Congress shall have power to enforce, by appropriate legislation, the provisions of this article.

(The Reconstruction Amendment, by the Thirty-ninth Congress on the 16th day of June, 1866, was declared ratified by the Secretary of State, July 28, 1868. The amendment got the support of 23 Northern States; it was rejected by Delaware, Kentucky, Maryland, and 10 Southern States. California took no action. Later, it was ratified by the 10 Southern States)

AMENDMENT XV

1. The right of citizens of the United States to vote shall not be denied or abridged by the United States or by any State on account of race, color, or previous condition of servitude.

2. The Congress shall have power to enforce this article by appropriate legislation.

(Proposed by the Fortieth Congress the 27th of February, 1869, and was declared ratified by the Secretary of State, March 30, 1870. It was not acted on by Tennessee; it was rejected by California, Delaware, Kentucky, Maryland and Oregon; ratified by the remaining 30 States. New York rescinded its ratification January 5, 1870. New Jersey rejected it in 1870, but ratified it in 1871.)

AMENDMENT XVI

The Congress shall have power to lay and collect taxes on incomes, from whatever source derived, without apportionment among the several States, and without regard to any census or enumeration.

(Proposed by the Sixty-first Congress, July 12, 1909, and declared ratified February 25, 1913. The income tax amendment was ratified by all the States except Connecticut, Florida, Pennsylvania, Rhode Island, Utah, and Virginia.)

AMENDMENT XVII

1. The Senate of the United States shall be composed of two Senators from each State, elected by the people thereof, for six years; and each Senator shall have one vote. The electors in each State shall have the qualifications requisite for electors of the most numerous branch of the State Legislatures.

2. When vacancies happen in the representation of any State in the Senate, the executive authority of such State shall issue writs of election to fill such vacancies: *provided*, that the legislature of any State may empower the Executive thereof to make temporary appointments until the people fill the vacancies by election as the legislature may direct.

3. This amendment shall not be so construed as to affect the election or term of any Senator chosen before it becomes valid as part of the Constitution.

(Proposed by the Sixty-second Congress on the 16th day of May, 1912, and declared ratified May 31, 1913. Adopted by all the States except Alabama, Delaware, Florida, Georgia, Kentucky, Louisiana, Maryland, Mississippi, Rhode Island, South Carolina, Utah and Virginia.)

AMENDMENT XVIII

1. After one year from the ratification of this article the manufacture, sale, or transportation of intoxicating liquors within, the importation thereof into, or the exportation thereof from the United States and all territory subject to the jurisdiction thereof for beverage purposes is hereby prohibited.

2. The Congress and the several States shall have concurrent power to enforce this article by appropriate legislation.

3. This article shall be inoperative unless it shall have been ratified as an amendment to the Constitution by the Legislatures of the several States, as provided in the Constitution, within seven

years from the date of the submission hereof to the States by the Congress.

(Proposed by the Sixty-fifth Congress, December 18, 1917, and ratified by 36 States; was declared in effect on January 16, 1920.)

AMENDMENT XIX

1. The right of citizens of the United States to vote shall not be denied or abridged by the United States or by any State on account of sex.
2. Congress shall have power to enforce this article by appropriate legislation.

(Proposed by the Sixty-fifth Congress. On August 26, 1920, it was proclaimed in effect, having been ratified (June 19, 1919—August 18, 1920) by three-quarters of the States. The Tennessee House, August 31st, rescinded its ratification, 47 to 24.)

AMENDMENT XX

1. The terms of the President and Vice President shall end at noon on the 20th day of January, and the terms of Senators and Representatives at noon on the 3rd day of January, of the years in which such terms would have ended if this article had not been ratified; and the terms of their successors shall then begin.
2. The Congress shall assemble at least once in every year, and such meeting shall begin at noon on the 3rd day of January, unless they shall by law appoint a different day.
3. If, at the time fixed for the beginning of the term of the President, the President elect shall have died, the Vice President elect shall become President. If a President shall not have been chosen before the time fixed for the beginning of his term, or if the President elect shall have failed to qualify, then the Vice President elect shall act as President until a President shall have qualified; and the Congress may by law provide for the case wherein neither a President elect nor a Vice President elect shall have qualified, declaring who shall then act as President, or the manner in which one who is to act shall be selected, and such person shall act accordingly until a President or Vice President shall have qualified.
4. The Congress may by law provide for the case of the death of any of the persons from whom the House of Representatives may choose a President whenever the right of choice shall have devolved upon them, and for the case of the death of any of the persons from whom the Senate may choose a Vice President whenever the right of choice shall have devolved upon them.
5. Sections 1 and 2 shall take effect on the 15th day of October following the ratification of this article.
6. This article shall be inoperative unless it shall have been ratified as an amendment to the Constitution by the legislatures of

three-fourths of the several States within seven years from the date of its submission.

(Proposed by the Seventy-second Congress, First Session. On February 6, 1933, it was proclaimed in effect, having been ratified by thirty-nine States.)

AMENDMENT XXI

1. The eighteenth article of amendment to the Constitution of the United States is hereby repealed.

2. The transportation or importation into any State, Territory, or possession of the United States for delivery or use therein of intoxicating liquors, in violation of the laws thereof, is hereby prohibited.

3. This article shall be inoperative unless it shall have been ratified as an amendment to the Constitution by conventions in several States, as provided in the Constitution, within seven years from the date of the submission hereof to the States by the Congress.

(Proposed by the Seventy-second Congress, Second Session. Proclaimed in effect on December 5, 1933, having been ratified by thirty-six States. By proclamation of the same date, the President proclaimed that the eighteenth amendment to the Constitution was repealed on December 5, 1933.)

AMENDMENT XXII

1. No person shall be elected to the office of the President more than twice, and no person who has held the office of President, or acted as President, for more than two years of a term to which some other person was elected President shall be elected to the office of the President more than once. But this article shall not apply to any person holding the office of President when this article was proposed by the Congress, and shall not prevent any person who may be holding the office of President, or acting as President, during the term within which this article becomes operative from holding the office of President or acting as President during the remainder of such term.

2. This article shall be inoperative unless it shall have been ratified as an amendment to the Constitution by the legislatures of three-fourths of the several States within seven years from the date of its submission to the States by the Congress.

(Proposed by the Eightieth Congress in 1947 and became effective on February 26, 1951, having been ratified by thirty-six States.)

AMENDMENT XXIII

1. The District constituting the seat of Government of the United States shall appoint in such manner as the Congress may direct:

A number of electors of President and Vice President equal to the whole number of Senators and Representatives in Congress to which the District would be entitled if it were a State, but in no event more than the least populous State; they shall be in addition to those appointed by the States, but they shall be considered, for the purposes of the election of President and Vice President, to be electors appointed by a State; and they shall meet in the District and perform such duties as provided by the twelfth article of amendment.

2. The Congress shall have power to enforce this article by appropriate legislation.

(Proposed by the Eighty-sixth Congress in June of 1960 and ratified by the 38th State, March 29, 1961 and proclaimed a part of the Constitution, April 3, 1961.)

AMENDMENT XXIV

1. The right of citizens of the United States to vote in any primary or other election for President or Vice President, for electors for President or Vice President, or for Senator or Representative in Congress, shall not be denied or abridged by the United States or any State by reason of failure to pay any poll tax or other tax.

2. The Congress shall have power to enforce this article by appropriate legislaion.

(Proposed by the Eighty-seventh Congress, August 27, 1962 and ratified by the 38th State, January 23, 1964.)

AMENDMENT XXV

1. In case of the removal of the President from office or of his death or resignation, the Vice President shall become President.

2. Whenever there is a vacancy in the office of the Vice President, the President shall nominate a Vice President who shall take office upon confirmation by a majority vote of both Houses of Congress.

3. Whenever the President transmits to the President pro tempore of the Senate and the Speaker of the House of Representatives his written declaration that he is unable to discharge the powers and duties of his office, and until he transmits to them a written declaration to the contrary, such powers and duties shall be discharged by the Vice President as Acting President.

4. Whenever the Vice President and a majority of either the principal officers of the executive departments or of such other body as Congress may by law provide, transmit to the President pro tempore of the Senate and the Speaker of the House of Representatives their written declaration that the President is unable to discharge the powers and duties of his office, the Vice President shall immediately assume the powers and duties of the office as

Acting President.

Thereafter, when the President transmits to the President pro tempore of the Senate and the Speaker of the House of Representatives his written declaration that no inability exists, he shall resume the powers and duties of his office unless the Vice President and a majority of either the principal officers of the executive department or of such other body as Congress may by law provide, transmit within four days to the President pro tempore of the Senate and the Speaker of the House of Representatives their written declaration that the President is unable to discharge the powers and duties of his office. Thereupon Congress shall decide the issue, asembling within forty-eight hours for that purpose if not in session. If the Congress, within twenty-one days after receipt of the latter written declaration, or, if Congress is not in session, within twenty-one days after Congress is required to assemble, determines by two-thirds vote of both Houses that the President is unable to discharge the powers and duties of his office, the Vice President shall continue to discharge the same as Acting President; otherwise, the President shall resume the powers and duties of his office.

(Submitted to the Legislatures of the fifty States July 6, 1965. Ratified by the 38th State (Nevada) February 10, 1967.)

AMENDMENT XXVI

1. The right of citizens of the United States, who are eighteen years of age or older, to vote shall not be denied or abridged by the United States or by any State on account of age.

2. The Congress shall have the power to enforce this article by appropriate legislation.

(Proposed to the States by Congress on March 23, 1971 and ratification completed June 30, 1971.)

III
APPENDIX
THE SUPREME LAW OF THE PLANET EARTH

No constitutions preventing governments from encroaching upon the rights of the people would ever be necessary if all mankind followed the basic instructions for the human organism. These instructions, found in the Babylonian Talmud (*Sanhedrin* 56-60), are addressed first to Adam, then to Noah; they have become known as **The Noahide Laws**. Essentially, there are only six laws (the word for six in Hebrew is *WAW*, the cognate for "law") in the Noahides; the Mosaic Ten Commandments, binding on Israel, were an unnecessary expansion of the Noahides. In fact, the chief complaint Christ lodged against the Pharisees (*Pharisee* = "Priest of Mosaic Law") was their strict obedience to a vast honeycomb of complicated written statutes.

You may wonder, as I have, why The Noahide Laws are nowhere listed in the Bible. I have no explanation. They are far easier to memorize than the Ten Commandments and, if observed, will make it impossible for you to break any of the Ten, nor any other law made in pursuance of the United States Constitution.

THE NOAHIDE LAWS

1. No idols.[1]
2. No blasphemy.
3. No murder.
4. No robbery.
5. No adultery.
6. No trial except by impartial jury.

---

1. No surrender of one's own self-respect to the authority of another. "Idols" include celebrities and dignitaries.

IV
APPENDIX
MATERIALS
FOR EDUCATING YOUR FRIENDS ON MAIN STREET

1

(Clyde Harmon of Mesa, Arizona, one of the pioneers of the enforcement of Article I Section 10, has used Affidavits like this one to exempt himself from paying property taxes in an unlawful tender. Any official granting a "taxpayer" permission to pay in something other than gold and silver coin would be perjuring his oath to support the Constitution. And without permission, how can we tender payment to the state?)

AFFIDAVIT

I, the undersigned, being duly sworn to support the Constitution of the State of _____ and the Constitution of the United States, do hereby grant permission to _____ to circumvent Article I Section 10, U.S. Constitution, so that he might pay his debts to the state in something other than gold and silver coin.

Dated this_____ day of_____, 198_____.

_____
Signature

_____
Name and Title

_____
Witness

_____
Witness

2

(Small businessmen may want to inform their customers that sales taxes are due only from those who wish to fuel the system that creates higher prices and higher taxes. Perhaps an announcement such as the one below taped to cash registers or bulletin boards would inform customers of the voluntary nature of taxes in an unlawful economy.)

NOTICE:
SALES TAX COLLECTIONS ELIMINATED

Since the currency of the United States is not redeemable in gold and silver coin, and since the United States Constitution forbids states and municipalities from making any thing but gold and silver coin a tender in payment of debts,

YOU CANNOT BE REQUIRED TO PAY SALES TAXES, and WE CANNOT BE REQUIRED TO COLLECT THEM FROM YOU.

If you wish to pay sales tax anyway (thereby helping to fuel the inflation of depreciating paper money), our Cashier will calculate the amount you owe as a free service. Then, you may mail your check or money order for that amount to _____
(State)

Department of Revenue, _____, _____.
(Address)   (Zip)

Yours truly,
THE MANAGEMENT.

3

TWELVE SIMPLE QUESTIONS TO ASK IN COURT, IN PUBLIC OFFICES, AND IN LETTERS TO OFFICIALS:

1. If I conspire with officials to violate Article I Section 10 of the Constitution and make something other than gold and silver coin a tender in payment of debts, can I be punished?

2. What is the punishment for conspiring with officials to violate the Constitution?

3. If I pay dollars, dimes, and cents of something other than the money of account of the United States into any public office, have I broken the law at 31 U.S.C. 371?

4. What is the punishment for breaking federal law?

5. Can a judge permit me to violate the Constitution?

6. Can a judge force me to help him violate the Constitution?

7. Can a judge force me to break a federal law?

8. If I break a law because a judge makes me do it, can I still be punished?

9. If a judge permits me to break one federal law, may I submit a list of other federal laws I would like to break, and would he permit me to break them, too?

10. If I broke a law requiring me to drive 55 mph on the Interstate, how come the judge gets to break a law requiring him not to make any thing but gold and silver coin a tender in payment of debts?

11. If I have to obey the law governing withholding taxes, do I have to obey the law requiring that I pay them in the money of account of the United States? If my employer withholds something other than the money of account of the United States from my paycheck, can I be punished for violating 31 U.S.C. 371? Can he?

12. If I can be excused from obeying the money-of-account law, can I also be excused from obeying the laws governing withholding taxes?

4
THE PAPER DOLLAR CAPER

Before 1963, Federal Reserve Notes, defined by law as "obligations of the United States" (12 USC 411), were "REDEEMABLE IN LAWFUL MONEY AT THE UNITED STATES TREASURY OR AT ANY FEDERAL RESERVE BANK." *Lawful money, you'll remember, "shall be construed to mean gold or silver coin of the United States." (12 USC 152.)*

After 1963, *the "REDEEMABLE" promise disappeared from the face of the Federal Reserve Note. But many redeemable notes are still in circulation. Since Congress has neither passed a law rescinding the redeemability of these notes into lawful money, nor changed the definition of "lawful money," the author maintains that all "REDEEMABLE" Federal Reserve notes ARE STILL REDEEMABLE IN GOLD AND SILVER COIN, dollar for dollar. Further, any state bank giving only paper dollars for them—rather than lawful money—is violating Article I Section 10, U. S. Constitution, by making something other than gold and silver coin a tender in payment of debt!*

In the 1960's, we learned complicated new technologies, overcame the complex barriers of outer space, acquired graduate degrees in unprecedented numbers. Our lofty minds, however, were unable to make sense out of the movements of a few simple words on and off our currency, movements that slipped private property from the pockets of us satellite-watchers gazing up into the ideasphere. . . .

IV: MATERIALS TO EDUCATE YOUR FRIENDS   145

The Silver Certificate was a U.S. Treasury receipt for one dollar's worth of silver, or 412.5 grains of silver 90% fine. Since it did not specify silver "coin," many Silver Certificates were redeemed for little bags of silver powder!

The irredeemable Federal Reserve Note was treated (and still is by many judges) as a "new kind" of Silver Certificate, when in fact it bears no relation in the real world to the Silver Certificate whatsoever.

To declare the Federal Reserve Paper Dollar to be a modification of the Silver Certificate is to perpetrate a fraud.

Yet, the Federal Reserve sent out the following press release[1] announcing the changeover:

FEDERAL RESERVE
press release[1]

For immediate release   November 26, 1963.

The Board of Governors of the Federal Reserve System and the Treasury Department announced today that more than 50 million new $1 Federal Reserve notes are going into circulation. Issuance of the new $1 notes, authorized by Congress last June, has already begun at all 12 Federal Reserve Banks and their 24 Branches to commercial banks in every part of the country. This will make more silver available for coinage purposes and help to meet the increased demand for currency in connection with pre-Christmas business.

To facilitate the widest possible distribution, the initial supply of the

---

1. C. O'Donnell, *The Standard Handbook of Modern United States Paper Money*, Sixth Edition, Harry J. Forman, Inc., Philadelphia, p. 28.

new notes is being distributed through normal commercial banking channels; none of the first 50 million notes will be available to the public at any of the Federal Reserve Banks or Branches.

The new $1 Federal Reserve notes clearly resemble the present $1 silver certificates, which ultimately they will replace completely. The back of the new notes and the portrait of George Washington on the face will be exactly the same as the silver certificates. The main difference will be the addition of a symbol, appearing to the left of the portrait, identifying the issuing Federal Reserve Bank, and the wording on the face of the bill. The notes bear the signatures of the Secretary of the Treasury and the Treasurer of the United States, as do Federal Reserve notes of other denominations.

The new notes will read [above the portrait]: "The United States of America" and [below the portrait] "One Dollar". The legend stating that the bill "Is Legal Tender For All Debts, Public and Private", appearing on the silver certificates will also appear on the new Federal Reserve notes, but the new notes will not contain any reference to silver. Thus, they will not carry the language: "This Certifies That There Is On Deposit In The Treasury Of The United States of America" [above portrait] and "One Dollar In Silver Payable To The Bearer on Demand" [below the portrait].

Federal Reserve notes have been the basic circulating currency of the United States for many years, comprising over 85 per cent [more than $30 billion] of the face amount of all currency in circulation today. They are backed 100 per cent by collateral in the form of gold certificates, U.S. Government securities, or short-term paper discounted or purchased by the Federal Reserve Banks.

Aside from Changing Times, *the only national magazine to mention the Federal Reserve's subtle issuance of irredeemable paper was U.S. NEWS AND WORLD REPORT, December 9, 1963. The event was treated like the introduction of a "new, improved" product. The logic is completely Alice-in-Wonderland: how does the* withdrawal *of silver certificates from circulation promote the coinage of silver dollars? Here's the U.S. NEWS story in its entirety:*

NOW, A NEW TYPE OF DOLLAR BILL

Fifty million $1 bills of a new kind are being put into circulation.

The new and old notes—as shown in photos above—are very similar. The major difference between the two is that the new bill contains no reference to silver. Congress authorized the Treasury to start withdrawing the $1 silver certificates so the Government's stock of silver bullion could be used for coins or other purposes.

If Congress approves, silver dollars are to be coined next year for the first time in 30 years.

5
The UNITED STATES
MONETARY SYSTEM

SUPREME AUTHORITY

Congress shall have power to coin money and regulate the value thereof, and no state shall make any thing but gold and silver coin a tender in payment of debts.

Article I, Sections 8,10: U.S. Constitution

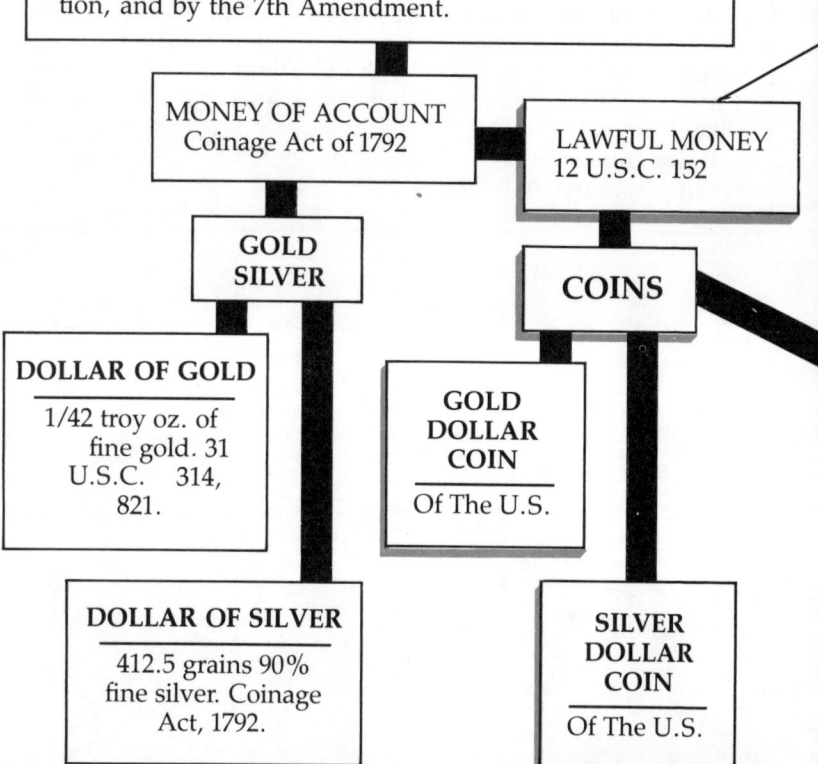

UNIT OF ACCOUNT OF THE UNITED STATES:
The **DOLLAR**,
permanently fixed by Article I Section 9, U.S. Constitution, and by the 7th Amendment.

MONEY OF ACCOUNT
Coinage Act of 1792

LAWFUL MONEY
12 U.S.C. 152

GOLD SILVER

COINS

DOLLAR OF GOLD
1/42 troy oz. of fine gold. 31 U.S.C. 314, 821.

GOLD DOLLAR COIN
Of The U.S.

DOLLAR OF SILVER
412.5 grains 90% fine silver. Coinage Act, 1792.

SILVER DOLLAR COIN
Of The U.S.

IV: MATERIALS TO EDUCATE YOUR FRIENDS 149

SOURCE: UNITED STATES CODE ANNOTATED

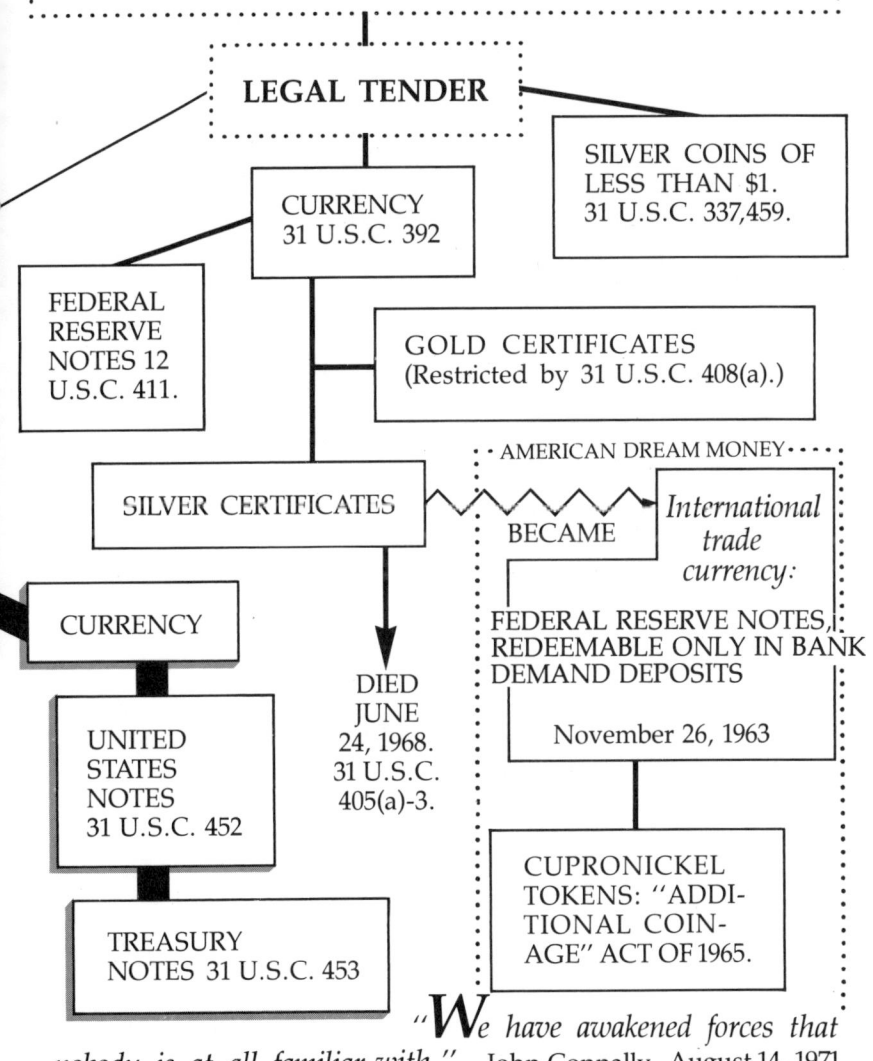

"**LEGAL TENDER**: That kind of coin, money, or circulating medium which the law compels a creditor to accept in payment of his debt, **when tendered by the debtor in the right amount.**"
Black's Law Dictionary, 5th Edition, 1979.

"*We have awakened forces that nobody is at all familiar with.*" —John Connally, August 14, 1971

6

Your Secretary of State will be happy to send you a copy of the Constitutional Oath of any officer in public trust. It gives me a feeling of great security having a copy of my public servants' pledges that they will protect my civil and economic rights and defend my family's peace and tranquillity.

STATE OF TENNESSEE

Oath of Office

I, John K. King, do solemnly swear that as Commissioner of Revenue for the State of Tennessee I will support the Constitution of the State of Tennessee and the Constitution of the United States, and that I will perform with fidelity and faithfully execute the duties of this office to the best of my ability. So help me God.

This the 20th day of January, 1979.

STATE OF TENNESSEE
COUNTY OF DAVIDSON

I, Houston M. Goddard, Judge of the Court of Appeals of Tennessee, have this day administered the Oath of Office to John K. King as prescribed and required by law.

This the 20th day of January, 1979.

V
APPENDIX
MORE SELF-ASSURANCE

(The following is excerpted from an astonishing July, 1980, AP release that never appeared in many American newspapers.)

DECISIONS EXPAND RIGHT TO SUE GOVERNMENT
By Richard Carelli
Associated Press

WASHINGTON—Although important decisions on abortion payments, racial quotas and the commercial use of genetic engineering attracted the most attention, the Supreme Court's 1979-80 term offered one overriding theme: **The expanding right of Americans to sue the government.**

In a half-dozen decisions on the government's liability to its citizens, the court lowered—or obliterated—centuries-old "sovereign immunity" barriers.

While seldom fodder for newspaper headlines, a citizen's power to hold government and its agents responsible for lawless actions is as essential to a republican form of government as is the power of the ballot.

In its just-completed term, the Supreme Court ruled:

• Persons whose constitutional rights have been violated can sue government officials directly under the Bill of Rights if Congress has not provided an "equally effective" alternative.

In the same decision, the justices extended the right to sue directly under the Constitution to cases involving violations of the Eighth Amendment's protection against cruel and unusual punishment.

• Persons can use an 1871 civil rights law [42 USC 1983, cited in Chapter 9] to sue for damages when **they believe some act by state or local governments violated a legal right** provided by Congress. Never before had the court given such broad meaning to that Reconstruction-era law, a major vehicle for the civil rights movement.

• Such lawsuits do not have to allege "bad faith" on the part of government officials. Instead, **those officials must prove they did not realize their acts were unlawful.**

• Local governments, unlike their employees, cannot get out from under a lawsuit charging violations of individual rights by proving the violations were unintentional or that the challenged acts were carried out in "good faith." The decision assured citizens whose rights have been violated the availability of some remedy or compensation.

• **State courts may be sued for damages** if they violate a person's civil rights in enforcing their administrative rules.

TUPPER SAUSSY
SEWANEE, TENNESSEE 37375

July 14, 1980

The Attorney General
 of the State of Tennessee
Capitol Building
Nashville, Tennessee

Dear Sir:

I am attempting to determine the validity of a judgment expressed in paper dollars, and am in need of an opinion from your office:

Is Article I Section 10, United States Constitution still binding on the states?

I thank you in advance for your prompt consideration of this question.

Sincerely yours,

(signature)

Tupper Saussy

State of Tennessee

OFFICE OF THE ATTORNEY GENERAL
450 JAMES ROBERTSON PARKWAY
NASHVILLE, TENNESSEE 37219

ATTORNEY GENERAL & REPORTER
WILLIAM M. LEECH, JR.

CHIEF DEPUTY ATTORNEY GENERAL
C. HAYES COONEY

DEPUTY ATTORNEYS GENERAL
ROBERT E. KENDRICK
EVERETT H. FALK
DONALD S. CAULKINS
WILLIAM B. HUBBARD
ROBERT B. LITTLETON
WILLIAM J. HAYNES, JR.

ASSISTANT ATTORNEYS GENERAL
WELDON B. WHITE, JR.
MICHAEL E. TERRY
DAVID S. WEED
ROBERT A. GRUNOW
JOHN A. GOEHRING
ROBERT J. AMES
LINDA R. BUTTS
DONALD L. CORLEW
FRANK J. SCANLON
KENNETH R. HERRELL
WILLIAM O. KELLY
JIMMY G. CREECY
HENRY E. HILDEBRAND, III
WILLIAM W. HUNT, III
ROBERT L. JOLLEY, JR.
CHARLES H. BARNETT
WILLIAM H. BARRICK
CLAUDIUS C. SMITH
ROBERT L. TUCKER
EDWIN M. WALKER
RICHARD S. MAXWELL
ROBERT L. DeLANEY
RICHARD S. DOUGHTY
JOE C. PEEL
MICHAEL J. PASSINO
KEITH JORDAN
CHARLES L. LEWIS
JOHN C. ZIMMERMANN
JOHN T. BUCKINGHAM
WILLIAM P. SIZER, II
JENNIFER H. SMALL
LEE BRECKENRIDGE
PERRY ALLAN CRAFT
AMELIA E. HENCHEY

July 22, 1980

Mr. Tupper Saussy
Sewanee, Tenn. 37375

Dear Mr. Saussy:

I am responding to your letter of July 14, concerning an opinion on the U.S. Constitution. I regretfully must inform you that this office is prohibited by statute from rendering legal opinions to private parties. <u>We receive several requests on this particular Article, and whether it is binding on states</u>, and the most I can offer is to refer you to a private attorney.

I am sorry that we cannot respond, but as explained above, the law does not allow us to. If I can be of any other assistance, however, please do not hesitate to contact me.

Sincerely,

Sheri M. Tigue
Administrative Assistant

RICHARD L. STRADLEY
ATTORNEY AT LAW
POST OFFICE BOX 97
WALNUT GROVE, MISSISSIPPI 39189

August 27, 1980

Mr. F. Tupper Saussy
c/o Spencer Judd, Publishers
Box 143
Sewanee, Tennessee 37375

Dear Mr. Saussy:

In response to your question "Is Article 1, §10 of the United States Constitution, particularly the words 'No State shall . . . make any Thing but gold and silver Coin a Tender in Payment of Debts . . .', still binding on a State?", the only lawful answer is Yes.

Meant to "crush paper money" by unanimous consent of the Constitutional Convention of 1787, this Section prohibits the States from imposing upon the people a paper currency, paper money or anything else other than gold and silver coin as a medium of exchange in the discharge of debts. Since the Constitution can be changed by amendment only, and since no amendment has changed this Section, no federal action can excuse a State of this prohibition.

The effect of this Section is thus:

If a paper dollar is delivered to, or received from a State-authorized party without particular objection to its being an unlawful tender under Article 1, §10, no Constitutional question has arisen, and the payor/payee, in remaining silent, has renounced his individual rights flowing from the Constitutional prohibition.

Those rights are the following:

A. Discharge of the debt in gold or silver coin, if provided for in the debt;

B. Dismissal or forgiveness of the debt altogether, if the debt is not denominated in gold or silver coin, since any rule or judgment repugnant to the Constitution is void, invalid, and without effect.

As with other rights, the right to gold and silver coin, and the right to be forgiven of any debt not denominated in same, are considered waived unless properly and timely asserted.

Sincerely yours,

Richard L. Stradley
Attorney at Law

RLS/ss

IN THE GENERAL SESSIONS COURT FOR ENTRAPMENT COUNTY,
RADAR CITY, TENNESSEE

STATE OF TENNESSEE,   )
    Plaintiff,   )
vs.   )   Case No. _____
)
    Defendant   )

MOTION FOR A DETERMINATION OF THE SUBSTANCE OF THE MONEY OF ACCOUNT OF THE UNITED STATES

Comes now the defendant, fearful that he might be poised to act in contravention of federal statutes, and petitions this Court to determine the substance of the money of account of the United States so that he can properly discharge the claim against him arising from this cause, and do so in compliance with federal regulations, paying in full and at law. In support of this Motion, the defendant shows the Court the following:

1. This Court is required to keep its proceedings in the money of account of the United States, to-wit:

> The money of account of the United States shall be expressed in dollars or units . . and all the accounts in the public offices and all the proceedings in the courts shall be kept and had in conformity to this regulation.   31 U.S.C.A.§371

2. Thus, the amount of dollars this Court ordered the defendant to pay are dollars "or units" of the money of account of the United States.

3. Defendant understands "dollar" to be not a coin or a piece of paper but the name of the unit by which monetary value is measured, just as "quart" is the name of the unit by which liquid is measured.

4. Defendant understands that the Coinage Act of 1792 declared gold and silver to be the money of account of the United States.

5. Defendant understands that 31 U.S.C.A. §408 prohibits the redemption of any United States currency into gold; further, that 31 U.S.C.A. §405(a)-3 prohibits the redemption of silver certificates into silver.

6. Defendant believes that 31 U.S.C.A. §408 and 31 U.S.C.A. §405(a)-3 prohibit him from paying any amount of dollars or units of the money of account of the United States, but seeks this Court to show him <u>with what Congress has replaced gold and silver as the money of account of the United States.</u>

7. If Federal Reserve notes or bank demand deposits (which, like the money of account of the United States, are expressed in dollars) have been declared by proper legislation to be the money of account of the United States, the defendant asks to be shown it, so that he can pay in such money, assured that he has fulfilled his obligation in full and at law.

WHEREFORE, the defendant, standing in ignorance and confusion, awaits the determination by this Court as to WHAT is the money of account of the United States that is expressed in dollars, and cannot act until such determination is made.

Respectfully submitted,

———————————————
Attorney for himself.

*T*housands of readers of the first edition of this book wrote their state attorneys general asking if Article I, Section 10 of the Constitution was still binding on the states. They received only silence, if not evasion.

Then Pat DiSalvo received this statement. Now, we have an opinion from the state itself upon which we can rely as we withhold payment of state-authorized debts denominated in something other than gold and silver coin:

TYRONE C. FAHNER
ATTORNEY GENERAL
STATE OF ILLINOIS
160 NORTH LA SALLE ST.
CHICAGO 60601

TELEPHONE
793-3500

February 24, 1981

Pat Di Salvo
3319 N. New England Ave.
Chicago, Illinois 60634

Dear Pat:

    In response to your letter, Article I, Sec. 10 of the U.S. Constitution is binding on the State of Illinois.

Sincerely,

Morton E. Friedman
Assistant Attorney General

MEF/mam

cc: File